ME TOO

A THERAPIST'S JOURNEY TO HEAL, FIND LIBERATION, & JOY

DEMARRA WEST

Published by Demarra West

info@demarrawest.com

Printed in United States of America

ISBN: 979-8-9896342-0-0 (paperback edition)

Visit www.demarrawest.com for additional information about this book

Dedication

This book is dedicated to my father who planted the first seed for me to write this book more than twenty five years ago. And my mother, who was part of the wellness movement long before it became popularized. I am me, in part, because of them.

Ashe',
Demarra

Contents

Acknowledgements

There are many people and life experiences that have contributed to the birth of this book, including anyone who has ever asked me to write a book over the years, championed me towards completing the book, or simply shared that my story impacted their life somehow. You know who you are! Major shout outs are due to the following, however:

Mom, thank you for all the time and energy you devoted to helping me get the story right.

Shelly Ryan, thank you for being an exceptional life coach who has supported me so fully towards the finish line.

Jem Muli, thank you for being a rock star executive assistant, and displaying a servant's heart with everything you do.

Zenda Lynette Thomas, thank you for your devotion to me, the work, and your unflinching pursuit of me completing the book.

Dr. Annice Fisher, thank you for telling me the world needs this book right now.

Deleath Blomberg, thank you for making room to edit this project in the midst of your rigorous schedule.

And last, but certainly not least, thank you Source/Universe/God/Creator for relentlessly sending me signs and wonders to get me here in spite of my many, many years of resistance.

Introduction

The Courage to Be Myself

Sue Patton Leolie, from her book The Courage to Be Yourself

I have the courage to embrace my strengths.

Get excited about life.

Enjoy giving and receiving love.

Face and transform my fears.

Ask for help and support when I need it.

Spring free of the Superwoman trap.

Trust myself.

Make my own decisions and choices.

Befriend myself.

Complete unfinished business.

Realize I have emotional and practical rights.

Talk as nicely to myself as I do my plants.

Communicate lovingly with understanding as my goal.

Honor my own needs.

Give myself credit for my accomplishments.

Love the little girl within me.

Overcome my addiction to approval.

Grant myself permission to play.

Quit being a responsibility sponge.

Feel all of my feelings and act on them appropriately.

Nurture others because I want to, not because I have to.

Choose what is right for me.

Insist on being paid fairly for the work I do.

Set limits and boundaries and stick by them.

Say yes only when I really mean it.

Have realistic expectations.

Take risks and accept change.

Grow through challenges.

Be totally honest with myself.

Correct erroneous beliefs and assumptions.

Respect my vulnerabilities.

Heal old and current wounds.

Favor the mystery of spirit.

Wave a goodbye to guilt.

Plant "flower" not "weed" thoughts in my mind.

Treat myself with respect and teach others to do the same.

Fill my own cup first, and then "nourish" from the overflow.

Own my own excellence.

Plan for the future but live in the present.

Value my intuition and wisdom.

Know that I am loveable.

Celebrate the difference between men and women.

Develop healthy, supportive relationships.

Make forgiveness a priority.

Accept myself for just as I am now.

I had no idea that when my father gifted me with these words more than fifteen years ago, five years before he passed away in a terrible freak accident, that they would come full circle in *Me Too: A Therapist's Journey to Heal, Find Liberation, & Joy*. That's the awe of the Source – that everything in our life has a purpose, which will be revealed in divine time.

My father was the first person to tell me I needed to write a book, and he remained steadfast about this until the day he took his last breath. So when I started to construct the *Introduction* it felt appropriate to begin with these words to help you ground into the journey you're getting ready to embark on.

My sense is you will want to return to these words many times over, as I have. They encapsulate every aspect of what it means to be a free woman, although any gender could benefit from keeping this message at the forefront of their life.

Me Too: A Therapist's Journey to Heal, Find Liberation, & Joy is twenty-six years in the making. When I write those words I'm really taken aback, and in fact it nearly takes my breath away. Not because I finally wrote the book, although I'm deeply proud of myself for accomplishing such a task, but more so because of everything that led me here. And the relentlessness of the Source/Universe/God/Creator to help ensure this body of work got delivered to you.

The day my father told me I should write a book I was sixteen. He and I returned from one of our go-to trips to Cracker Barrel to feast.

When we arrived back at my apartment, he insisted he walk me to the door. Him walking me to the door wasn't odd, but the way he said it felt different than any other time which, in part, explained the silence between us as we approached the door. When we reached the top of the porch steps, he grabbed my hand and said, *"Daughter, I need to tell you something. You need to write a book. You've been through so much in your life and you could be an inspiration to so many."* I stared intently in his eyes as these words rolled off his tongue, and even when he was done I couldn't seem to take my eyes off him, let alone respond. My trance was broken when he asked me if I heard what he said. I told him I did, and was grateful that he saw me in that way. We exchanged a hug, expressed our love for each other, and went our separate ways. He brought it up on several occasions after that but I always brushed him off, never allowing the thought to enter my stream of consciousness.

And then when I was twenty-six I started feeling the urge to write, but was quickly deterred when I went back to my childhood friends to recount things that happened and they refused to help me. Trauma had done quite a number on my memory, so many details that I thought would be important to include in my book I couldn't access. I didn't realize that would be a pivotal moment of me starting to face myself and the remnants I had left behind because of the trauma I had endured.

As time went on, between the rejection of those I called on for help and the rigor of writing, I stopped writing altogether. Then a couple years later I started again. And would restart over and over and over again, over the course of fourteen years.

There were times that I would write profusely, for example, when I completed an 80,000+ word manuscript during *National Writers Month* back in 2008, along with a book proposal, and pitches to more agents and writing awards than I care to remember. This merely resulted in being put on a short list for a single writing award. And then there would literally be years when I would write absolutely nothing at all.

I knew deep down that writing a book was my destiny. But when it was all said and done, I also knew this book would change everything in my world, and although change has been a constant in my life, this kind of change felt massively different. I felt it at a cellular level, and to be completely honest with you, it scared the shit out of me.

I didn't know if I was emotionally strong enough to tell stories connected to my trauma and grief. I also didn't know if I was ready for the world to see me completely naked due to my deep sense of privacy. Although I had obtained a master's degree in clinical mental health and believed in the power of healing through "storytelling," had written countless blogs for my work with *Be Well Beautiful Woman*, and had only told my truths–this was still vulnerability at a fairly surface level. The kind of vulnerability that it would require to write about my experience with gang rape, molestation, domestic violence, and more, would force me to enter into a different realm of exposure, not just for myself, but people that I cared about profoundly, like my mother.

In spite of this, Source/Universe/God/Creator was relentless in not letting me forget writing a book was part of my light work. As a result, no matter what I did, or how much I accomplished, the book wouldn't escape me. It would come to me in my dreams. It would come to me in visions that people had about my life. Random people at random places for years have shared that they overheard conversations connected to some of the stories I'm going to share in this book, and felt deeply inspired. Countless friends and associates have inquired non-stop about me writing a book—even those who had no idea a book was in the works.

And just last year my elementary school pen pal sent me a message on Facebook with all the writing I sent her when I was ten years old. I connected with this woman years before when she was my daughter's program director at a private school she attended. Upon meeting her, neither of us had a sense that our paths had ever crossed before and then, late last year, more than seven years from the time we first met, she queried me about my maiden name. I simply assumed we had gone to grade school together. And then she tells me we were pen pals. Not only that, she had every letter I had ever written to her. And I had absolutely no recollection of ever having a pen pal. The gift of my words at ten years old, I knew, was no coincidence. It was one of those loud and clear signs urging me to complete the book.

And now back to the poem...when I first read the words framed in plywood the color of light sand, surrounded by blush and blue roses bunched in clusters, they touched me deeply. Not just the words themselves, as they alone have immense power, but the fact that my father, who had been absent much of my life, somehow still *knew* me.

During the last eleven years of his life, before he was taken from me on his way home from visiting his hometown of Bastrop, Louisiana, we had many moments of *knowing*. Times when he would expose the most vulnerable parts of himself, and I to him. I never articulated the unsettling I felt with my life during this time, but he felt it, and acknowledged that he knew, without actually saying it. He would simply utter, *"Daughter, it's going to be alright."* I can't tell you how many times he reassured me that all would be well. That was his go-to phrase for the underlying void I felt that was fortunately visceral only on a few occasions. Those five words provided temporary comfort that would carry me until the next time the feelings would push their way back to the surface. My father, who had, for the majority of my life, caused me great pain, had somehow become my solace.

I didn't know then how deeply unhappy I was, and that it was mainly connected to the trauma I had experienced as an adolescent. I had thrust myself into my education, healing the world, being a wife and mother, and that shielded me from the truth: I too had immense work to do to heal myself. Never once in my clinical training had I believed that healing was my work. I believed that there was nothing to heal. I had left that life behind and had become an upgraded version of myself. What happened to me as a child and through my teens was over. I did an exorbitant amount of external work to separate me from my past–obtaining a master's degree, entrepreneurship, founding a not-for-profit, and volunteering, and yet the wounds of my past were still present.

When I look back over the years through my current lens of healing, I realize there were countless signs that I was suffering. Moments when I was so depressed that it debilitated me from doing almost anything. Times during my first year of marriage when I would have flashbacks of my gang rape causing me to physically reject my husband–resulting in weeks of not being sexually intimate. As time went on these feelings subsided, but I rarely ever initiated sex, and outside of when sex was involved, I barely touched Curtis. It wasn't that I wasn't attracted to my husband–I found him to be very handsome–but my body remembered that tragic night and it was blocking me from having the intimacy I subconsciously desired. As open as my heart was in service to the world, there were parts of me that were shut off.

In the fifteen years I was married, I can count on one hand the number of times friends were at my house. Outside of my professional world and family, I lived in a bubble. Curtis, my daughter, and I in the historic house that was built in 1864 that I just had to have as soon as I laid my eyes on it. I thought I was happy in this bubble. Well, I was at least content there. I was keenly aware of moments when I would flounder between melancholy and downright sadness, but I would tune in to all the ways that Curtis was good to me, which were plentiful, and that would move me back to a place of gratitude for what was.

Even in my fairly close relationships, they would do much of the talking, and although I didn't lie about my life, I also didn't share many details. I was comfortable being in the role of listener because that meant I could shield parts of myself and create connection with no real depth. I had no consciousness of this, in fact, if you had asked me then I would have told you what an open book I was. I honestly believed that my friends were simply taking up space because they were selfishly leaning on their therapist friend, but in actuality they were taking up so much space because I took up so little. I longed for depth and yet I was unwilling on many levels to provide it. At that time I wasn't ultimately capable of depth, because it would have meant that I was capable of vulnerability which my trauma had mainly stripped from me.

In spite of all this, my life was good in many, many ways. I traveled across the globe on a regular basis. I loved being a mom. I was deeply grateful I had a partner that I could rely on. Curtis always allowed me to be myself, and he never, ever tried to control me. He supported my friendships, the times I'd want to travel alone, and everything I set out to do in my life. He even wholeheartedly embraced my family, at one point taking on the role of helping raise my niece and nephew.

Curtis relished in taking care of me and our daughter and was committed to defying many traditional gender roles to make full space for us. He did most of the cooking and gladly cared for our daughter during the evenings when I was taking night classes during graduate school.

Nevertheless, I felt disconnected from my life, myself. The spiritual base that I was being fed didn't align with my beliefs anymore, so just five years into my marriage, I stopped going to church. I woke up one day and told Curtis that I simply couldn't do it anymore, and from that point forward I never went back. The church had been part of my life for as long as I could remember. I got married in a church, went to premarital counseling at a church, and served in the puppet ministry for years as an adolescent. The church was so important to my grandmother, who would say nearly every time you saw her, *"You know I'm keeping you in that Psalm 91,"* that the first thing she would ask about when she met someone new, was what church they went to. But it no longer fit, and I was no longer willing to try to make it fit, so that was that.

The more I achieved, the more education I received, the more my business grew, the more I served in my community, the more I started to feel disconnected to Curtis, too. I was evolving at the speed of light, while he remained in nearly the same spot he was when we got married. He had been promoted at work, increasingly made more money and was an exceptional father and husband, but he was perfectly content with life exactly the way it was. I thought I, too, would be okay if he remained the same. At least I said that during premarital counseling when I was asked by the pastor if nothing changed with Curtis could I see myself being with him for life. At the time, that was a resounding yes for me. What I hadn't predicted though is that my expansion would ultimately change my mind, and that from there a series of unfortunate and fortunate events would occur that would bring me back home to myself.

A place that I never knew was missing because my trauma started at such a young age, and therefore I started to separate from my true essence too early to recall anything different. My labor was my home—it was the one thing I had always been able to control. That was one of the reasons I excelled as a student. No matter how chaotic the world around me was, no matter how many times I was told to shrink as a child, or that my pain and suffering wasn't valid, I could create my own world of validation in concert with my educational environment.

I worked my ass off to achieve—which paid off in many ways—but at the cost of being overweight, so stressed that my hair was thinning, and many sleepless nights.

Embodying the fullness of Leolie's poem is something we all have to fight for daily, but if you have experienced trauma that fight becomes that much more challenging. Our joy, peace, and purpose are rooted in our ability to own each aspect of who we are. That is, the truth of who we are, along with the ways we've been harmed by the world or done harm to ourselves or others.

Liberation represents pure power and a return to our true nature, which is that we are whole simply because we are born. There is absolutely nothing we have to do to prove that we are worthy. Our worthiness is rooted in simply coming into the world. And yet, from childbirth, we absorb a plethora of messages telling us we have to be something we are not in order to be accepted, especially when trauma is present.

That process of shrinking can be quite exhausting, not to mention, every time we represent in ways that aren't really who we are, we are giving our power away. Our power to choose our own pathway, what is ultimately best for us, what is deeply calling us, what is truly aligned with us.

I have read the *Courage to Be Myself* countless times over the years, but it wasn't until ten years after I was given the gift of the words, that I actually allowed them to take hold of my life by beginning to center healing. This is rooted in the *Course in Miracles* teaching which says, *"When the student is ready, the teacher will come."* I had knowledge about every element of the poem and yet in practice I was falling short. Knowledge, at the end of the day, is only powerful if we allow it to become part of who we are, but that can't happen until we are truly ready for it to take hold.

Where I began on this journey is so far removed from where I am today, not just in terms of my healing as a complex trauma survivor, but all the ways I've liberated as a Black multiracial, pansexual woman that grew up in poverty. My understanding of what it means to be truly well has also changed drastically since my formal training as a therapist shaped my initial perspectives. And although I still believe in the power of therapy, I now have a vast understanding of creating well-being from the inside out, and that we don't have to wait on anyone, or anything, to begin and continue the healing journey.

Wellness practices have taught me that the more we ground into ourselves, the more we can live our lives fully, and attract the very things we want, and with ease—no matter how much darkness seeps its way into our lives. Meditation, Reiki, yoga, spending time in nature, laughing, and simply relishing in life provides the foundation for healing, liberation, and living well overall.

That embodied understanding is a homecoming, since technically my mother planted those first seeds of wellness, long before things like retreats and juicing became popularized. We owned a huge bright yellow juicer and we would have to drink whatever concoction of carrots, radishes, celery, and more that she conjured up. We never had a sweet thing in the house. Our snacks consisted of rice cakes. We rarely ever ate anything fried. Our cabinets were bare much of the time but she always provided a hot meal. She even left us with her friend Lanna when I was ten to attend a retreat center in Arizona.This was not just rare for the times, this was rare for a poor, multiracial woman.

The stories that felt most important to write for myself first, and then for the world, have also changed drastically. There was a time when I was harboring a victim mentality which caused me to position myself as, well, the victim, and everyone else as the villain. Because of my thorough understanding of trauma now, and the years of concerted work I've done to heal myself, I understand the humanity in us all more clearly which has hopefully humanized each character in my story whose actions caused me harm, including myself.

So here I am, twenty-six years after my father planted that first seed, telling my sacred stories of intense pain, redemption, and liberation through indigenous healing practices that have helped me not only heal, but curate an abundance of joy, peace, and financial wealth.

These stories were written for survivors, but also those who have the sacred responsibility of helping survivors heal, including educators, therapists, law enforcement, and more. This book is dedicated to helping them understand the power their actions have to set survivors on a trajectory of healing to find solace in the midst of a storm or deeper suffering.

The first section of *Me Too: A Therapist's Journey to Heal, Find Liberation, & Joy* is devoted to helping you understand complex trauma and my individualized relationship to it. The second section highlights the most significant traumatic events that I experienced while the third section explains the aftermath of the trauma and how it impacted my adolescence. The next section is the beginning of my liberation. And the final section highlights the practices that not only helped me to heal, but also supported me in creating a life rooted in abundance - on a mind, body, spirit level.

My sincere hope is that my life's testament will change the lives of those who have endured trauma, helping them face the parts of themselves that have been difficult to look at, talk about, and fully own. It is also my hope that these stories and practices will help individuals co-create the life they truly deserve by helping them understand the sheer power they have to work with Source/Universe/God/Creator to manifest their deepest desires. Not just for themselves, but for the people they're destined to share their light with.

I also hope that by the end of this book individuals understand fully that life is unfolding for them, constantly helping them see and hear the things they need to know in order to become their truest and highest selves. That we know we're always being guided and protected. And the only real work we have to do is the work within to be fully present to the beauty of life in order to engage in sustainable liberation, transformation, and consciousness building.

The moment we recognize that Source/Universe/God/Creator is always speaking to us, we can be at ease, releasing to what is and pivoting accordingly. Because at the end of the day, who we are, and what we become, is ultimately up to us and Source/Universe/God/Creator will follow suit.

Trauma & My Connection To It

Chapter 1
Trauma & My Connection To It

Trauma has been part of my DNA since I was six years old. Well, I should specify conscious complex trauma, which simply means the first memory I have of something that deeply hurt me and, therefore, dramatically shaped me. Trauma started long before that though, based on the way I witnessed my stepfather mistreating my mother. But honestly, I don't have memories of the abuse at that time, more of a sense–and a knowing–when I became an adult, imparted to me by my mother about the verbal, emotional, and at times, physical abuse he terrorized her with. The first distinct memory I have of him being abusive would come four years later, when I was ten.

But the incident that occurred when I was six . . . I remember some of those details quite vividly. And after it happened, I recall wanting to tuck myself away, desiring not to be seen, not necessarily in physical form, but more so, the burden that now lay on the inside of me. The shame I felt was potent. It was the beginning of me not just telling secrets, but living in secret. That sexual trauma invoked by my mother's friend's son, Duke, who was our babysitter, was the beginning of a childhood riddled with confusion about my sexuality, low self-esteem, body shame, and disconnection from myself–inhibiting me from being able to experience my body's natural design to experience pleasure.

As stated in the book *Push*, by Sapphire, although my mind knew these moments with Duke felt off, I didn't *really* know otherwise, in part because of the physiological effects of sexual trauma that don't exist in other forms of trauma. This makes the impact deeply layered and quite challenging to heal. It's why children who've been molested, or people who have been sexually assaulted, often report life-long remnants associated with the trauma. Mentally you know the act of being sexually abused isn't right, yet your body responds in a positive way–the way the body was designed to when being sexually stimulated. This often creates deep shame for survivors.

Not to mention, the person who typically commits the sexual act is someone you have positive feelings towards which means they have a level of influence over you, especially if you're a vulnerable young child. This is what makes predators so good at what they do. They gain access through close relationships with the family or as a result of their profession and coerce children through goods, services, and lies. This is also why incestral sexual trauma is so complicated, that is when a sibling, often older, is committing sexual acts on a younger sibling. You love this sibling dearly, and often look up to them, so although you understand on some level that the act is wrong, there is deep conflict. And often the sibling causing the sexual harm is also harming the other sibling in additional ways, which could be threats, or even physical harm, to maintain control in order to continue carrying out these acts.

Before I go any further in my personal relationship to trauma, in order to ensure we have a baseline understanding, I want to flush out some key definitions and outline trauma's impact, particularly as it relates to children.

An estimated 70% of adults in the United States have experienced a traumatic event at least once in their lives. *Trauma*, as I have come to understand it as a clinical mental health therapist and Trauma Center Trauma Sensitive Yoga (TCTSY) certified practitioner, which is the first evidence-based yoga program designed for the treatment of psychological trauma, *is a result of exposure to a single incident or series of events that are emotionally disturbing or life-threatening with lasting adverse effects on an individual's functioning and mental, physical, social, emotional, and/or spiritual well-being.* And although anyone can be traumatized at any age, the impact on children has a more pervasive, long-term impact.

There are three main types of trauma based on this definition. *Acute trauma* is a result of a single incident involving things like a car accident or physical or sexual assault. Even witnessing these kinds of events can cause us to be acutely traumatized.*Chronic trauma* on the other hand, is when repeated and prolonged abuse is happening, such as domestic violence or physical, sexual, or emotional abuse. And again, just witnessing these events can be chronically traumatizing, as in the case of a child seeing a parent being abused by another parent, or a sibling observing another sibling being abused, even if they are not being abused themselves, as we heartbreakingly witnessed in *Netflix's The Trials of Gabriel Fernandez*. Sometimes, the siblings not being abused act abusively towards the sibling that is, seemingly for their own protection, to partner with the abusive parent. And lastly, **Complex Trauma**, also called **Complex Post Traumatic Stress Disorder (CPTSD)**, is exposure to varied and multiple traumatic events, often of an invasive, interpersonal nature, and in repetition over a prolonged period.

And although **CPTSD** can affect adults, it is actually more present in children, at an estimated three percent to be exact, which is the same rough percentage of people with traditional **Post Traumatic Stress Disorder (PTSD)** which develops in reaction to physical injury or severe mental or emotional distress, such as in military combat, violent assault, natural disaster, or other life-threatening events.

The point that I made about children being most affected by trauma is of critical importance because of the devastating long-term effects it has on their developing brains, hearts, immunity, and overall development. This can present itself in frequent colds, hyperactivity, acts of physical and verbal violence, and in worst cases, heart disease later on in life.

To help us have a deeper appreciation of what this means for children like myself, who grew up with CPTSD, meaning having many trauma factors at play–some for prolonged periods of time–we're now going to briefly examine **Adverse Childhood Experiences (ACEs)** which are traumatic events that occur before a child reaches the age of eighteen based on research done between 1995 and 1997 by CDC-Kaiser Permanente. This research explored the impact of trauma on physical and mental health problems in over 17,000 adults.

4

What they identified were ten ACESs that are correlated with negative behavioral and health outcomes that include:

1. Physical abuse
2. Emotional abuse
3. Sexual abuse
4. Physical neglect
5. Emotional neglect
6. Mental illness
7. Incarcerated relative
8. Mother treated violently
9. Substance abuse
10. Divorce

When a child has more ACEs, they have a stronger correlation to things like heart disease and diabetes, poor academic performance, and substance abuse later in life. When you couple this lived experience with things like racism, community violence, and unsupportive adults, **toxic stress** sets in which can have irreparable damage to the brain and body. In other words, stress becomes harmful or toxic when there is no safe haven available to support the healing process, which causes the stress in our bodies to dwell within, on a cellular level, affecting so many major organ systems in the body. Additional examples of how trauma can present itself on a mind, body, spirit level include:

- Memory loss or confusion about the event
- Alternating between feeling emotionally numb and experiencing intense and intrusive emotions
- Re-experiencing or re-imagining the traumatic experience
- Avoidance of reminders of the traumatic experience or what was lost in the experience
- Hypervigilance or a constant state of arousal
- Aggression
- Disruption of identity

And there isn't one of these that I haven't experienced since that first traumatic experience. In fact, memory loss and reimagining the trauma still play out in my life to this day. This is why it's problematic for individuals to feel that if trauma happened in the past it's no longer valid. Trauma lives in the bodies, minds, and hearts of those who have been impacted by it for life. The pain becomes less over time, through the choice to heal as a means to be as free as we can from it, but it becomes a part of our fabric. Freedom from trauma is never truly achieved. We just learn to live with it, liberate ourselves from it, and thrive in spite of it.

Although everyone experiences stress, and some stress is good, giving us motivation to make important changes or solve problems, if we're experiencing anything other than a *positive stress* response, which is the body's response to temporary stress helping the body do what's needed in the moment and then regulating once the event passes, our body begins to go into a state of emergency. For example, if a child were to fall and hurt themselves, this would be considered *tolerable stress* which requires a caregiver to help soothe the child until they can get back to their normal stress level. This is why acknowledging any sign a child is distressed is important–it allows them to bounce back faster if there's a caring person there to act as a buffer. Even if they're truly physically hurt, the love shown by the caregiver offsets this pain, making the child feel more secure again. Let's say in this example the caregiver ignored the child, or punished them for displaying emotions because of the fall, or simply told them to "suck it up," then the child experiences *toxic stress*, which, as I shared, happens when the body can't turn off its stress response normally. This pattern–on repeat–causes lasting stress that can harm a child's body and brain and cause lifelong health problems.

ACEs research has shown that more than 66% of the population, regardless of income, have experienced at least one ACEs, and nearly 25% have experienced three or more. I had eight ACEs by the time I was twelve. Plus I am a woman of color, grew up in poverty, and although many people attempted to help me when I started to "act out" around the age of thirteen, their tactics only made things worse, and left me feeling misunderstood, rejected, and unloved. And those feelings lingered for years. I even coined myself the "black sheep," in part to buffer those feelings, not just within the context of my family, but in life.

It wouldn't be until close to my seventeenth birthday, after experiencing all kinds of hardships, like substance abuse, incarceration, and homelessness, that I even started to become open to changing or healing. And although four years of having deeply painful experiences may not seem like a long time, when you're a child in the midst of toxic stress, and that stress eventually causes you to be at war with yourself and the world, every moment you're engulfed in this unbearable pain feels like an eternity. So, for four of my teenage years I was a walking zombie at best, and obsessed with dying at worst.

Now back where I started; when that first sexual encounter happened at six years old, although I know it happened I can't actually remember it. Yet this knowledge lives in my body. During traumatic events, one can not only dissociate during the trauma itself, but maintain this dissociation, causing you to forget the gory details of the traumatic act. One can remember the surroundings, many details leading up to and following the traumatic event, but can block the act itself out altogether.

Dr. Lauren Fogel, a psychologist from Allina Health put it this way, "Dissociation is a form of freezing. We often hear the term flight or fight response. There's a third, less well-known called the freeze response. It's an automatic mechanism the body goes into without conscious thought." Research has shown that people in traumatic situations can concentrate so much on surviving that they don't pay attention to the part of the brain that consolidates memories. And because there is no conscious thought associated with the incident, trauma, at times, can be out of sight and out of mind, sometimes never coming to the surface.

I can see Duke and the setting we were in when it happened. I remember my brother and sister being in the living room with us. I recall the position of the television playing cartoons in the corner of the room, and how the light was muted. It was dark outside. I can remember how the noise from the cartoons ceased to exist as I followed Duke up the stairs and went into his room. He closed the door behind us. I remember it being dark behind that closed door, but everything else I have no recollection of. Not the conversation that led me to go up the stairs with him, whether my siblings came to see what I was doing, or what happened after the door was closed and he was done doing whatever he did to me. I vaguely remember going back into the room where my siblings were still enjoying cartoons. I have no recollection of my interactions with them, or quite frankly how I felt or the thoughts I had once rejoined with them. I also don't remember going home, or even thinking much about the incident after that night Duke molested me. I didn't conjure up the words to tell a soul either, until one day I witnessed my mother getting ready to hang out with Duke's mother, and I lost it, having a full-fledged emotional breakdown, spewing what little I could recall about the incident that happened more than eight years before.

Although I have no concrete memories of the abuse itself, this trauma literally lives in my body, is stored in my cells, as Bessel van der Kolk describes in *The Body Keeps the Score*. This is why talk therapy is so limited when it comes to helping trauma survivors, and therapy that includes somatics, or movement, energy work, or priming our mind towards abundance, can take us much further in our healing. All of those healing and mindset modalities help us release blocked energy, in this case involving trauma, allowing renewed cellular energy to be produced, and the healing process to take root.

I'll talk more specifically about each of these forms of healing in the book, but I would need many books to explore, in depth, my lived experiences aligned with ACEs, leading up to my healing, so instead I'll chronicle the events that had the greatest impact on me in the next section, *My Trauma Chronicles*.

MY TRAUMA CHRONICLES

Chapter 2
God Let Her Live

God, let her live. These were the words my mother called out to Source/Universe/God/Creator when she thought she was going to lose me. I wasn't the first child she had lost and although she certainly mourned those children, she said the moment she felt like she was going to miscarry me, those words, which were hers, but felt like someone else's, came through. My siblings she lost before me weren't any less important than I was, but for whatever reason she felt led to fight for me in this way.

My mother and father met while she was working to complete her degree in nursing at Western Michigan University (WMU) and was living off campus in family housing. She had gone out to a nightclub with friends, diligently trying to get her mind off a Nigerian guy, who was also a student at WMU. She had dated him for several months and broke it off with him because his wife, whom he planned to divorce, was now pregnant with their second child. This was devastating to my mother who had envisioned that they would be together–a family–and now that wouldn't be so.

My father, on the other hand, was separated from his childhood girlfriend, Dalma, whom he had bolted from Bastrop, Louisiana with after discovering her family would be moving to this place called Kalamazoo, Michigan. He was fifteen at the time and had endured so much pain–both within his family, and from the community at large–

that he left the first chance he got. In the years before he left, Dalma's mother often had my father over for meals since she knew the poor conditions he was being raised in, not to mention the way he was being mistreated by his stepfather. I'm convinced that if it hadn't been for Dalma's family, he would have potentially starved, and been at even greater risk of being harmed by men in Bastrop, who took advantage of his abject poverty, and neglect, by forcing him to do unspeakable things in exchange for little money so he could do basic things like eat.

My father was charming, handsome, and could light up the room with his laughter, but he wasn't very nice to my mom during the mere six months their relationship lasted. He never physically harmed her, but he was emotionally abusive and worked actively to make her feel less than. Not just through the number of times my father cheated on her, or how he pretty much came and went as he pleased–sometimes not communicating with my mother for days at a time. Or even that he was hard pressed about getting back with Dalma with whom he had my sister, Charminique a couple years before. It was the way he actively spoke down to her, telling her things like she could never achieve what she expressly desired, such as completing nursing school. My mother is convinced this was because he had never dated anyone like her before, not just in terms of her academic pursuits, but also her complexion. My mother is light, light, light, and has Eurocentric features because of her bi-racial identity which made her the target of immense colorism for her entire life. In one respect, she wasn't "white" enough and in the other respect she wasn't "black" enough, making her the center of "othering" at every turn.

So when my mother was left alone in her apartment on New Years Eve, on the dawn of 1980, all glammed up and dressed in black from head to toe, with gold accented jewelry, staring out a window in a plush yellow chair with armrests, waiting for my father to pick her up and he never came or called, that was it for her. For hours, she just sat there in silence, with the light subdued; just her, the yellow chair, the window draped in velvet curtains with big yellow flowers, and emotions so heavy it felt as if she was going to sink. With her body slouched over, and tears streaming down her cheeks, she whispered to herself, *"Please help me."* Shortly after she spoke those words, she heard Source/Universe/God/Creator say, *"I'll never leave you nor forsake you."* which startled her, but when she heard it again, and then again a third time, she was able to receive the message. That gave her the courage to get out of that chair and start again.

Within a few days after she kicked my father out, my mother found out she was pregnant. When she ejected him from her life she thought for sure that would be the end of their relationship which is ultimately what she wanted. She had grown to despise him, and was convinced he despised her too. Now she would be attached to him for life because of me. This was challenging for my mother in general, but also because she had pretty much been on her own in raising my sister, Dayo. Now she also had this strained relationship with my father and would be bringing his child into the world which would make her responsible for raising two children now—mainly solo.

Nearly eight months later, to term, I came into the world. Eight pounds, six ounces of me to be exact, which was the biggest baby my mother ever delivered. I caused her to gain a whopping eighty plus pounds, which crazily, was on par with my weight by the time I delivered my daughter. During my mother's pregnancy, my father and she spoke a few times on the phone but he never came to see her or participated in any way in her birthing journey. Even when she went into labor he was nowhere to be found. And when he finally made it to the hospital he merely dropped off flowers, making no contact whatsoever with either of us.

By the time my mother hired an attorney with the little money she had—and with no support from legal aid—she took my father to court based on his refusal to pay child support, he had seen me a whopping two times. When the judge ordered him to pay a meager $50 a week in child support, he made clear to my mother how angry he was about it, although he had never done anything for me financially.

In spite of that, my mother was shocked when my father didn't come to the hospital that tragic day I went into emergency cardiac surgery at the age of two, due to the growth of an extra valve that was cutting off my blood supply. It was my stepfather, Jettie, who had married my mother about six months prior, who was there. When I came out of surgery, my mother decided she would no longer make an effort to have my father in my life. In fact, she preferred him not to be involved based on the fact she had no desire to have me exist in a world where I was treated with so little love and care. She wouldn't keep me from him, but she was also done trying.

The first memory I have of my father would be nearly eight years later when I was ten. He picked me up in his shiny blue Cadillac which stood out among the cars in the public housing townhome community in Oshtemo Township where my mother was only paying $46 a month for rent.

I remember how handsome he was–how the sun hit his flawless almond skin. His smile just drew me in. He had the straightest, whitest teeth that looked like milky white Chiclets and illuminated ever so brightly. He was wearing a dark blue Adidas silky jumpsuit with blue and white matching shell toes. A white Kangol and a chunky silver chain like Run DMC wore in the videos topped it all off. I was mesmerized by his beauty. In fact, I couldn't take my eyes off him.

Years later I discovered I too had those teeth, and a host of other things, like my fathers bone structure. I can hear my Aunt Dumi saying, *"Girl, you look just like your daddy."* For years I resented this because deep down I resented him and the way he had mainly cast me aside. He had his life, which seemed to be worlds away from mine, and I had mine.

As we walked to the car, my hand in his hand, I skipped. I caught a glimpse of my shadow. I loved seeing my twists wrapped in clear knockers with yellow plastic bow barrettes dangling on the ends of my hair, which had a tint of red in the sun, bouncing up and down to the pace of my skips. I liked my yellow and black polka dot outfit–a skirt and biking shorts bottom, with a cat that had bright pink lips and a pink bow draped over my chest. I felt pretty. I wondered if my father felt the same when he looked at me.

As I got closer to the car, I noticed people were inside. I hadn't heard him say that anyone was coming with us. Just when I caught the nerve to ask who they were, he started to speak.

"I have a surprise for you. Oh, you're going to love this! You just wait!" "But, daddy . . ." I wanted to tell him I didn't want to wait; I wanted to know now before we got to the car, but he was already opening the car door. *"Demarra, I want you to meet your sister, Diata. And this here is her mother, Joy."*

I glanced at Joy for a second and then my gaze stayed plastered on Diata. My father stood at the door staring at us, more so me, for what seemed like minutes, and then said, *"Aren't you going to say hi? This is your little sister. She's your family. Go ahead and say hello. Don't be rude."* I wondered why he was putting so much pressure on me to engage with Diata. And he had referenced my silence as rude. I wasn't the only one being silent. Plus I had no recollection of ever spending time with my father and this is how he decided to come back into my life?!

"Hi." is all I could manage to say. *"Alright now, was that so hard? Get in the car, and put your seatbelt on."* said my father as he hopped in and did the same. Once the ignition was turned on, he turned to Joy, kissed her on the cheek, and said, *"See baby, they're going to get along*

just fine. It's going to be a great day! Ain't that right girls?!?!? (as he looked in the rearview mirror at Diata and me). *Just one happy family. And we about to have some fun today."*

I examined every inch of Diata as we rode to the Kalamazoo County Fairgrounds. She looked a lot like my dad. I always thought I was the only one who so succinctly resembled him, and although I had resentment about this I was glad, deep down, that this was one thing that couldn't separate us. I didn't like that Diata looked like him, as much, if not more than I did, but yet as I saw her, I saw myself. *"How could I despise the very thing I am?"* I thought. As I pondered this question, I also took notice of how well Diata, Joy, and my father were dressed. Although I loved my outfit, it looked like hand-me-downs in comparison to their attire. I felt out of place–like somehow I didn't belong.

I had countless questions as we rode to the Kalamazoo County Fair which I was elated about. I discovered they lived in Chicago. And Diata was three. That my father would drive to Chicago a couple times a month to see them or they would periodically come into town. If that was the case, why hadn't I met them before? Why did it take him all this time to allow our worlds to intersect? Why had he been spending all this time with them, while he gave me absolutely none of his time? I boiled with anger as the journey continued, but I had learned to mask that so I sat in silence for the rest of the journey. Ultimately I was just grateful to have another sister.

The fair was something I always looked forward to. Although we didn't have a lot of money, my mother somehow found a way to conjure up enough for my siblings and I to get on a couple rides or play some games, and have at least one treat, like cotton candy, which was like eating pure magic. When I heard my father say we could ride on anything, and play any games we wanted, even if that meant repetition, I couldn't believe what I was hearing. I had never had unlimited access to anything as a child. My mother simply couldn't afford it. Even on the rare occasions she would allow for food indulgences, I had to share. If we went to McDonalds, for example, I'd get one hamburger and a handful of fries from a large fry and a cup of orange drink from the large size, because it had to be split amongst myself and two siblings. If we went to Taco Bell, my mother would get a family pack, which meant I got my own bean burrito, but the chips and cheese and cinnamon twists would be rationed with my brother and sister.

So when my father followed with, "And you can eat whatever you want, and as much as you want." I thought he was really full of it so I said, *"Dad, really, anything we want is up for*

grabs . . . you have the money to pay for anything we want?" He said, "Yes, daughter, so go, enjoy yourself. Take your little sister, keep an eye on her, and here is twenty dollars for you all to get started." I had never held a twenty dollar bill in my hand, let alone had the responsibility to spend it. Babysitting, well, I had plenty of experience with that, and had even started to watch a toddler for one of the single moms that lived in my townhome community to make money.

Still apprehensive though, I said, "Dad, are you sure? This is a lot of money." "Yes, daughter, I trust you. Plus I know how your brain works. You're smart, good with math, so you've got this. Now go on. I won't be too far if you need to find me. And don't let your sister out of your sight."

Hand in hand with Diata and her favorite doll clenched by her side, we started to walk away. I looked back at my dad on a few occasions but he didn't notice because he was too busy being engulfed in whatever Joy was saying, so on we went.

As I walked away, I became increasingly annoyed. My feet kept moving one in front of the other, and I could feel Diata's hand, but my mind was elsewhere. *What did he know about my math skills? Although he was right, he hadn't been around and had no right to say that. I was good at math but I wasn't just good at math I was good at everything in school. I got 100% on my MEAP test which is rare I'm told, but where was he? I got an award for the poem I wrote that was plastered all over the city. Why didn't he come and see me read my poem at the Kalamazoo Institute of Arts? Doesn't he know how special those moments are? How special I am? I'm also in the academically talented program for math and English, but he wouldn't know any of this because he simply hasn't been here. Why hasn't he been here? He must not love me. Why doesn't he love me?*

Diata tugged at my arm, and said, *"Sissy, did you hear me? I want to stop here. You're not listening." "I'm sorry. Sure we can stop."* I looked up and realized we were at a snack place that served popcorn, cotton candy, and corn dogs. I liked that Diata called me Sissy. I enjoyed being a big sister. I wonder if Dayo felt like that. All of a sudden I was missing my real sister, well, at least the only sister I had known.

Diata and I landed on cotton candy–blue for her and purple for me–and we continued walking as we allowed the cotton candy to melt into our mouths. We walked slowly through the fair grounds searching for what we wanted to do next. I kept Diata close, but our hands were free so we could fully enjoy our treat. Periodically we would stop to take in the sights and the sounds. This seemed to distract me for a few minutes, but then my mind drifted back to my father.

And he just has money to throw away like this? In his flashy clothes, with his beautiful, perfect girlfriend, and Diata . . . without me? I hate him. I absolutely hate him. Doesn't he know I'm struggling, that we're struggling? Does he even care? Of course he doesn't. If he did, he would have been here. It wouldn't have taken him ten years to show up in my life. And he thinks he can take me to the fair one time, and all will be well? No. It's not fair. It's just not fair.

I stopped dead in my tracks and the tears started to silently flow as I clenched Diata's hand. She asked what was wrong over and over again, but I was unable to speak, and my feet seemed to be planted in the ground so I also couldn't move. Then all of a sudden I snapped out of it, wiped my tears, reassured Diata I was fine and we kept it moving, getting on every ride we could until it was time to go.

By the time we saw my father and Joy again, the sky was filled with darkness and the droves of people that had been there when we arrived had mainly dispersed. My dad greeted us with that same smile he seemed to always wear. I wondered if this was his constant expression, but I had no way of knowing since I hadn't been around him. As we walked to the car, my hand in Diata's and my dad's hand in Joy's, I wondered when the next time would be that I would see my father.

Although my dad asked Diata and me if we had fun when we first got in the car, once he was reassured with our yeses, the remainder of his focus stayed on Joy as we drove back to my house. When he parked, I gave Diata a hug, told Joy "Bye," and my father held me by the hand as we walked up to my door. I didn't want to go, and I didn't want him to go. I held the tears back because I didn't want him to see me cry. When my mom opened the door, my dad knelt down to hug me, kissed me on my check, and said he would see me soon.

"How soon?"

"I'm not sure, daughter, but soon."

"Do you promise?"

"Yes daughter, I promise."

"Soon like next week?"

"Maybe not next week, but soon."

"Okay."

My mother looked at me before she said goodnight to my father and closed the door. I rushed to the window to watch him walk to his car. I kept watching until the car was no longer in my sight, and even when it was gone I kept staring out the window. The tears flowed as I just stood there in silence. My mother remained close by, and asked me how my night was. I simply said, *"Fine."* while still looking at the window. She prodded, but all I could conjure up was, *'It was fun."* as I continued to look out the window.

"It's late, Demarra. I'm glad you had fun. Let's head up to bed."

It took me a few moments before I could respond. I didn't know why, but I didn't want to leave the window.

"Demarra, come on, really, it's time for bed."

I wiped my tears before I turned to face her and simply said, *"Okay."*

Once in my room, tucked tightly under the covers, I cried silently. It would be months before I saw my father again, and even then, the absence of his time would still be present.

Chapter 3
The Wrath of Jettie

The early years after my stepfather Jettie came into our lives is a blur to me, but there are countless pictures of me with him where I look deeply happy. One of which stands out. We were at a park and Jettie was sitting on the grass with his midnight body leaned up against a tree, wearing a red shirt with black mesh sleeves and a black leather sailor hat. It's sunny, and I'm frolicking in my bare french toast body with the exception of my bleached white underwear. I'm running towards him with our arms extended towards each other, as we wait for what I presume will be an embrace. I had to be maybe two at the time

Of course this is not a moment I remember but this is how I want to remember Jettie. There were innumerable moments like this where Jettie was being loving, fully present, with his deep laughter or singing that could fill an entire space. What lingers though is the sheer havoc he wreaked on our lives. Although he never overtly hurt me or my siblings, the things we witnessed, and those instances when my mother would leave him, had major implications on us. There were also times when we weren't just observing the abuse or fleeing from his rage, but moments when we were a direct casualty.

Like during my tenth birthday party. Before I blew out my candles on the cake my mother made with pink frosting and eleven blue candles with horizontal white lines - one of which was to pay homage to the following year - opened my presents, or finished my first slice of pepperoni pizza, Jettie forced himself into the house in an intoxicated, and probably high stupor which scared off my six friends who were celebrating with us. Luckily, they lived in the complex and could quickly and safely get home on their own. The more my mother asked Jettie to leave, the more irate he became, resulting in him removing everything from the table with immense force. He eyed the record player playing Stevie Wonder's *Master Blaster* and quickly thrust it against the wall. Before he slammed the door on his way out, he muttered all kinds of profanity under his breath about how no good my mother was.

When it was all said and done, the table that was once carefully decorated with a pink tablecloth and matching plates, cups, and silverware in honor of my special day ceased to exist. Remnants of those items, the slices of pizza, and the cake my mother put her heart into, were on various parts of the beige carpet in the dining and living rooms and splattered on the eggshell walls.

My mother and I sat in silence for a while, her on the gray couch with her head slumped over, and me at the mahogany dining room table sitting with a straight posture, staring directly ahead, as if waiting to be served by someone. I took myself back to moments before when my friends Josie, Natasha, Marta, Lauren, Maribella, and Nicole were with me. I imagined us together, picking up where we left off. They sang *Happy Birthday* in unison and when they were done I made my wish . . . before blowing out my candles, and receiving the celebration of clapping afterwards. As we enjoyed cake and ice cream, laughter, and banter, I felt love. I wanted this feeling all the time. *Why couldn't I have this feeling all the time?* Anger started to boil to the surface, but before it could take full form, I heard the sound of my mothers voice.

"Demarra, why wouldn't you respond to me?!"

"What? Sorry mom. What did you say?"

"I said go pack your things."

"Pack for what?"

"We're leaving."

"Why?"

"Because I don't feel it's safe for us here."

"But I don't want to go."

"Well, you have to."

"But mom . . ."

"There is no but. I said go pack. Do it now. We have to leave soon. I don't want to be driving late at night."

"Mom please I just want to stay home, sleep in my bed."

"Demarra, I'm not going to tell you again. We don't have time for this. Now go pack. You have five minutes."

I stormed out of the dining room before I stomped up the stairs to my room and slammed the door. As I looked around my room, at the few belongings I had, it made me not want to leave even more. Tears ran down my cheeks as I packed my purple cloth suitcase, covered with *My Little Pony* stickers, to the brim. I had no idea how long we would be gone, and didn't want to ask because I had no interest in talking to my mother. I figured I would simply take as much as I could, including my favorite baby doll whose milk chocolate complexion was the same as Dayo's. She wore a baby blue leotard with sheer blue tulle and hot pink skates. I took her with me everywhere I went.

I can't remember anything after that. Not driving the two hours to Ypsilanti. Not staying the night with my grandmother's friend Arlene and her family. Not leaving Arlene's to go to a women's shelter. Not checking into the women's shelter where we stayed for a week. Not even coming back home to the mess Jettie left us. Absolutely nothing.

But what I do remember is the immense sadness I felt. The love I once had for Jettie, the only father I had come to know that had been facilitated by family trips, going to the park, watching television, and laughing and singing had started to fade. I had always despised the way he treated my mother, but this was something altogether different. The truth was, I wasn't just mad at Jettie, I was angry with my mother. No, I was heartbroken that she allowed Jettie to come back into our lives over, and over, and over again, no matter what he did.

When Jettie first came into my mother's life, she had high hopes about what her life, our life, could be. In the beginning it appeared that things were turning for the better. He took an active interest in my sister, Dayo, and me. He claimed to be supportive of her dream of finishing her nursing degree at Western Michigan University. Jettie had a great job that provided an ample income. He even owned a house and two cars. And he doted on my mother in a myriad of ways. A year later they were married and things quickly started to change.

Jettie controlled all the money. Even if my mother wanted to go grocery shopping he would have a prewritten check for what she needed. And although periodically we would go on excursions together as a family, for example to Cedar Point amusement park, he provided only the basics for my mother and our care. Even when my brother, Jonbenet, came into the picture a couple years after they were married, this control didn't let up. He did, however, spend more freely when it came to Jonbenet, and it also seemed he could do no wrong because whenever my mother would attempt to discipline him, Jettie intervened. So not only did he have strict reign on all the finances, he controlled her every move when it came to my brother.

My mother's dream of completing her degree would be squandered as well. Jettie made it clear he wasn't going to support her going to school anymore, even if that simply meant keeping us while she was in class. She was also forced to get a job and figure out our care, so she could have her own money. All the while Jettie is living large, spending "his" money freely, at times even hosting parties where he would generously provide alcohol, marijuana, and sometimes cocaine to his guests.

When Jettie and my mom first started dating she knew he enjoyed going out, they met at a bar, after all. She didn't know how much, however, and didn't understand that it involved things other than alcohol and marijuana. Although my mother had tried marijuana, she didn't like the way it made her feel and only drank on occasion because she also didn't like the way alcohol affected her energy level and digestion. Not to mention she liked to feel like she was in complete control. This increasingly caused tension in the relationship because she didn't like the idea of us being exposed, in any way, to drugs—especially ones that could have a direct impact on us, like smoking.

What I thought would be the last time my mother left Jettie, we were coming back from a trip up north–Peloton Village to be exact, to visit family. My mother and Jettie started to argue. The more my mother tried to end the conversation, or tell Jettie to calm down, the louder he became. At one point he gripped her arm. My mother tried to wriggle out of his grip but he seemed to clench harder. When he finally removed his hand from around her arm, his fingerprints still lingered in the form of a huge bruise which lasted for days. For fear of all of our lives, when he stopped at a gas station, she took my siblings and I into the bathroom. When Jettie walked into the gas station, my mother gathered us and fled to the police station that was within view. Shortly after we arrived, we were escorted to the Women's Resource Center of Northern Michigan where we stayed for a week before moving in with my grandmother.

As soon as we returned to Kalamazoo, my mother called Evergreen South, a townhome community in Oshtemo township, and got on a waitlist for Section 8 housing. When they told her that it would be a three year wait she didn't flinch. It didn't matter that the wait list was three years long. She had the long game in mind.

Most of that period is a blur to me; so much so that much of my recollection of what had actually taken place was not quite accurate. For example, I remember that we visited my grandmother during this time versus the truth, which was that we lived with her for months before my mother got back into family housing on Western Michigan's University's campus.

There is one distinct memory I have during those three years before we were informed we could move into Evergreen South. On this particular day, my siblings and I are in the living room, which is where we slept. It was the wee hours of the morning and we were still under blankets and beginning to rise from our slumber. My grandmother was making coffee in the kitchen and when she walked back in the living room towards her room, we caught sight of her butt through her nude pantyhose. My grandmother always wore nude pantyhose, no matter how hot it was, or what she was wearing– including pants–and now we knew why. What started out as faint laughter turned into full belly laughs making it obvious how grossed out we were that our grandmother didn't wear any underwear. I can still see her chastising us for this, but as soon as she left the room our laughter continued, along with the days that followed.

The next thing I remember is the day we moved into Evergreen South. Dayo and my mother went back to Jettie's to pack up the rest of our things. After the car was packed with everything that could fit, they commenced to leave. Before making it out of the driveway, Jettie snapped and threw a large garden sculpture that resembled cupid through the window of the car, which shattered the entire windshield before my mother managed to get away. All the while Jettie is yelling at the top of his lungs. *"You can't take my car. Oh, you're just going to leave me here and think you can take my shit? You no good . . ."* Although I wasn't with them that day, I overheard my mother and grandmother talking about it.

I was filled with excitement when we arrived at Evergreen South. One of the first things I did was ride my purple Huffy bike with a white basket, purple hand grips, and iridescent purple and pink streamers that seemed to fly in the wind when I rode. As I cruised through the complex I was in awe. There were three play sets, endless sidewalks to ride my bike on, a huge field for running or playing soccer, a basketball court, a forested area full of pine trees, and a pool.

As time went on I discovered blackberry bushes planted at various places throughout the complex which I often indulged in and a gas station where I could get penny Tootsie candy that was just a short walk once you got through the forest.

For the few years that followed it seemed we were in the clear from Jettie's wrath. Then that dreadful day on my tenth birthday happened. It wasn't too long after Jettie took up residence with his friend Kacela who lived only four units away from us in the same complex—a mere three to five minute walk. This was odd in general, but also because Kacela's son Wamai was my friend with whom I spent a lot of time playing. It seemed as if we were all at the mercy of Jettie.

Jettie's motives for moving in with Kacala seemed to be a ploy to get my mother back, She, however, was dead set on building a better life for us by pursuing her bachelor's degree, working, dating, and limiting her contact with Jettie exclusively to matters regarding my brother, Jonbenet.

Dayo and I were glad to not have Jettie in our lives, but Jonbenet was determined to get them back together, often pleading with my mother to give Jettie another chance. Wanting so desperately to be a "complete" family and not wanting Jonbenet to grow up without a consistent male presence, my mother decided she would give him another chance. Jettie promptly left Kacela and comfortably took up space in our lives again. For a while things were good. Then my mother got pregnant.

The night we found out the news that my brother, Jimuyu, would be coming into the world, Jettie and my mother were caught up in a verbal fight which quickly turned violent. His screams lured Dayo, Jonbenet, and me upstairs where the commotion was. As we entered my bedroom, Jettie's more than six foot frame had backed our mother into a corner as he hovered over her calling her every profane word ever created about women. Her head was sunken down as tears were rapidly falling from her cheeks, saturating her white lace nightgown. Through her tears, she begged Jettie to stop, but he kept at it. Even when she pointed out how upset we were, he wouldn't let up and instead directed his words toward us.

"She's so weak. Look at her tears. Only a weak person would be crying like this."

"You know your mom's a whore, right?"

"She's worthless. What a sorry excuse for a woman."

"She blames me for everything wrong in our relationship, but she's the real problem."

"You know your mom's no good, right?"

And then he directed his attention back to my mom.

"Tell them you're a piece of shit."

"That you're no good."

"That our relationship is broken because of you."

"Tell them. I said fucking tell them."

"God damn it, if you don't tell them what a lying, sad excuse of a woman you are, I'm going to slap the shit out of you."

"I said tell them, you bitch."

My mother refused to respond, but her sobbing never let up. Up until that point, Dayo, Jonbenet, and I had maintained a safe distance from Jettie because we too were afraid. Our bodies were shaking as we cried, begged, and pleaded for him to stop. No matter how much we tried, he kept on with his rampage.

And then he said, "I should just kill you. Be done with you for good. End both of our misery. You're such a sorry excuse for a human."

My world cracked and something came over me. I started to walk towards Jettie slowly, spewing commands that didn't feel like my own.

"Get your hands off her."

"Please don't do this."

"You're hurting her, can't you see that?"

"Just stop–please, just stop."

"You can't kill our mother."

"Get away from her."

"Leave, please leave. Leave us alone."

When I got to Jettie, I started tugging at his arm to get his attention. As the words flowed from my mouth, saying some of the same commands over and over again, my siblings followed suit in near unison, but stayed in the same place I had once dwelled. After what seemed like an eternity, Jettie stopped talking and locked eyes with me. My words, however, didn't stop flowing from my mouth nor did my grip or gaze. His focus shifted sullenly to my siblings for a brief moment, then back at me for seconds before redirecting his attention to my mother again.

"Good thing you're pregnant with my child. Because if you weren't, well, who knows how this could have turned out." And then he turned to look at all of us again. "Oh yeah, that's right kids, your mom is pregnant. And you know what, she was going to get rid of it. My child. Your sibling. This bitch was actually going to kill it. Congratulations."

He walked out the room, down the stairs, got his keys, and left the house. It would only be a matter of weeks before we saw Jettie again, and we picked right back up from where we left off as if we were one happy family.

Jettie remained in and out of our lives for the rest of my mother's pregnancy. When she delivered Jimiyu, he came to the hospital and stayed with them until she was released. As in the past, my mother slowly, but surely, allowed him to ease fully back into our lives. Until Jimiyu was the age of two things seemed to be fairly peaceful. I witnessed several occasions where Jettie acted loving toward my mother. He was actively contributing time and money to help out. This was the first time since they had been married my mother had experienced Jettie as generous when it came to matters of us. This provided hope that we would finally be the family she always wanted. Then Jettie became addicted to crack cocaine.

My mother had recently graduated with her bachelor's degree in business administration. Her dreams of becoming a nurse had dissipated because of the rigor of such a degree, mixed with the struggles and lack of support she had in raising the four of us. It took her fifteen years from the time she started at *Western Michigan University* to the time she graduated from Davenport University to get that degree. Shortly afterwards, she got a job with the State of Michigan in Lansing, which would have provided her with the income she needed to finally get us out of public housing. She and Jettie talked about the job and what it would require. The only way this would work was if Jettie kept Jimiyu while my mom was working, which he said he would happily do.

On her first day of work Jettie was missing. By the time he appeared, my mother would have only been slightly late for work, but instead of giving her the car, they had an altercation, and he threw her keys in the woods. Unfortunately she wouldn't find her keys until hours later since they were buried in the myriad of leaves that had fallen to the ground, causing her to miss her first day of work.

She was perplexed by his behavior considering the last couple years and the fact they had discussed the job thoroughly. As she pondered what had just happened, she came to the realization that she couldn't rely on Jettie to provide the support she needed to keep the job, which would have drastically changed our lives. So she called and resigned. What she didn't know then was that Jettie was struggling with drug addiction and it was about to rock his world.

That was it for my mother. She never took Jettie back after that. Jettie's life quickly spiraled out of control. He was fired from the good job he had. The cars he had once coveted had been repossessed. The house in Oakwood was foreclosed. And nearly every possession he had once owned was now nearly non-existent.

The last time I saw Jettie as an adolescent, was when Jonbenet and I went to visit him in a one room apartment he was staying in. Upon our arrival, his speech was distorted and his large frame had dissipated, leaving mainly skin and bones. He was wearing light blue hospital scrubs which he seemed to drown in since he had lost so much weight. The tiny pale yellow room with no decor on the walls housed a twin bed that took up the majority of the space, a side table that held a pack of Newports, and a velvet gray chair that held a few of his belongings. The only thing that was familiar to us was Jettie's baritone singing and laughter. And that would have to be enough.

Chapter 4
Night Crawlers

I always looked forward to Fridays. Hanging with my friends was one of the ways I escaped the reality of my life. This Friday would be extra special since I would go to Max's to hang out. We had talked on the phone for weeks. He even gave me his dark green leather Green Bay Packers jacket late one night in the graveyard directly across from his house. It happened to be chilly that evening which was odd considering it was still summertime. Even in the Midwest having a cold summer night was rare. I had never been particularly fond of football, but I liked the effort I felt Max was putting forward. I also liked the way the jacket fell on top of my shoulders. The weight of it made me feel safe.

The sky was like that painting I saw once at the Kalamazoo Institute of Arts called *The Starry Night* by Vincent van Gogh. Each time I thought about the painting, I could imagine it as if I was there, staring at it again for the very first time.

The energy between Max and me was something I hadn't felt before. I mean I liked him–*really liked him*, but the increased beat of my heart and the jumping in my belly–that was new. I couldn't be sure that Max felt what I was feeling, but I allowed myself to consider the possibilities.

There were so many things I liked about Max. He was a lot more mature than the guys I went to middle school with, which I guess made sense considering he was three years older than I was. He was nice, attentive, funny, edgy–he had this bad boy persona like Johnny Depp which had been a crush of mine ever since I first saw him on *21 Jump Street*. Even though Max was still living with his father he was able to do things most guys his age couldn't do. In fact, he moved through the world as if he was an adult renting a room from a perfect stranger. Anything went at Max's–at least that's what he told me.

I was fascinated by this kind of freedom. I longed for it for quite some time. That longing began the moment I started to feel like the black sheep in my family. No matter what I did to gain the attention of my family, it never seemed to amount to much of anything. Eventually I simply stopped trying and drew inward hopeful that my feelings of despair and isolation wouldn't overtake me.

The freedom at my home was mostly limited to the confines of the gated community we lived in. This was great when I was a child, especially during the summer when my siblings and I would wake up at the crack of dawn, eat whatever we could find in the pantry–which was usually dry unsweetened cereal and milk–and sprint out into the warm sun. It didn't matter if we hadn't bathed or even in some cases if we were wearing the same clothes as the day before. The zest I used to feel for the place I called home now ceased to exist.

It was difficult for me to focus on my studies when my thoughts were filled with seeing Max. Lately, he was all I could think of. So often in my classes, I'd doodle his name with purple ink and place a heart next to it over and over again. Or I'd be looking out the window thinking about where Max was, what he was doing, if he was thinking of me. This started to affect not only my grades but also how my teachers saw me. One white male teacher who taught AP English pulled me out of class one day to inform me that I would be better suited in a non-AP class. I was one of two Black students in the class at the time. Up until that point, I had been a model student. I was taking advanced classes, tutored other students, and handed in assignments on time. I always brought home good grades. I scored 100% on spelling tests. A poem I had written won a *Kalamazoo Institute of Arts* award and was plastered on the inside of city buses for the world to see. I had even gotten 100% on the Michigan Educational Assessment Program exam which was rare. And I read so much that I never missed the chance to get a personal pan pizza through the *BookIt* program. And now my studies and how that would open the door to a better future couldn't be further from my mind.

As soon as the bell rang, I bolted to my locker to gather my belongings and walked as quickly as possible to get to the bus. I tenaciously looked for Zurina but she was nowhere to be found. I desperately wanted to tell her my plans to stay at her house so I could go see Max. She knew I liked Max, but wasn't very supportive of that fact. Every time I brought him up she would drill me with questions. No matter how well I responded to her interrogations she maintained her position: *Max was no good for me.*

Max had dropped out of school, sold marijuana, and there were rumors he had sex with lots of girls, but there was way more to him than those things. His mother abandoned him when he was quite young. She was still around periodically but his father mainly raised him and his brother, Nate. I could relate to his pain of abandonment. He had built up so much resentment towards his mother, that a few years prior he attempted to drown her at the beach. He convinced her he was playing when she finally came up for air, but deep down he hoped she didn't live. The rage he felt didn't scare me. I often felt similar rage underneath the surface. And when he told me that I was the only person he had ever admitted that to, it made me feel like what we had was special.

I entered the bus alone since Zurina was missing in action. Students continued to file into empty seats until the bus was nearly full. The bus driver instructed everyone to sit down and announced he was getting ready to take off. Just as we were going to pull off, I noticed Zurina running towards the bus. I was relieved as I didn't know how I would be able to pull off my plan without her. As soon as our eyes met, she saw me beaming and she simply shrugged which signaled her confusion about my demeanor. I waved my hands indicating for her to hurry up. She rolled her eyes as she always did when she thought I was being dramatic. Zurina plopped down and groaned loudly. I decided that my news could wait since she clearly needed to talk.

"What's wrong?"

"Uuuugggggghhhhh; I could just kill Ms. Hill! I really think she hates me. Every time I do anything in class she calls me out. What is it about me? Do I have an invisible sign on me that says, 'It's okay to fuck with Zurina?' Gosh!"

"I'm sorry you had such a crappy day! I don't know why she insists on targeting you. I am so glad I am not in any of her classes! But again I am sorry that you have to deal with her."

"Can you get someone to kill her for me so she can get the hell out of my life? Just joking! No, I'll be okay. I just had to vent. I can usually deal with her shit, but today she really got to me!"

"Is everything else okay?"

"My mom has been such a bitch lately. She is never home, and I am so sick of dealing with her boyfriends. God, I just wish she would put me first for one time in her life! Why is it that I always have to babysit my little brother when she goes out all night to be with the guys she's dating? It is her responsibility, not mine!"

"You have a right to be upset. You are always watching your brother for her. She acts like she is the child and you are the parent. It boggles me that adults can be so fucking clueless about being parents."

"I know, right?!?!"

"Okay, so now it seems like it's okay for me to tell you what I was so excited about. I want to go to Max's tonight and I want you to go with me."

"Hell no. I'm not going and I don't think it's a good idea for you to go. He is such an asshole! I don't know what you see in him! Yes, he is cute, but what else? There has to be more to a guy than just being cute. He knows that girls fall over backwards to be in his presence. He will hurt you, Demarra! Don't go! You deserve better than him!"

"I think you're being too harsh on Max. I told you all that shit about his mom leaving his dad. I think he is really hurt from all that. Plus neither of us knows if he is even seeing anybody else right now."

"Yes, but have you even asked him about other girls, where your relationship is going, what he sees in you?"

I sat speechless. We had been friends since we were in second grade so she knew my silence meant that on some level I agreed with her, but she also knew when I made my mind up about something that was pretty much the end of it. I valued her opinion though and desperately wanted her to not only side with me but to also go with me so I wouldn't be alone. When she wouldn't budge, I was silent for the rest of the bus ride. Serious doubt started to creep in. I couldn't admit this to Zurina though. I was afraid that if I let on she was right, then it would give her the fuel she needed to convince me not to go see Max. As soon as we arrived at Zurina's I tried to change her mind.

"So, you're not going to come with me? You're really going to make me go all by myself?"

"You're not going to make me feel guilty for not going. I told you how I felt. I told you not to go. If you choose to go, it will be on you! Don't come crying to me when he hurts you!"

"That's cold, Zurina. You can be so goddamn mean sometimes. I get it. Fine, you won't go with me. That's fine, but don't expect me to do anything with you when you want to. Isn't that what friendship is all about? You doing what your friends want to do and vice versa?"

"No—not when it involves doing things that you disagree with. Demarra, I love you. You are my best friend. Friendship is about being honest about shit like this. If you can't take it, I'm sorry."

It was 9 p.m. on the dot—the exact time that Max told me to call and verify our plans.

"Hey," I said, trying to sound cool.

"Who's this?" he inquired.

I hated when this happened. I hoped that for once when I called he would recognize my voice—especially because we had been talking for weeks now.

"It's Demarra," I said calmly.

"Oh, what's up?" he said.

Trying not to sound disheartened I said, "Are we still planning to get together tonight?"

"Yeah, I guess that's cool. I don't have any plans. When are you coming through?"

"I'm not sure. I don't have a ride and don't have money to take a cab. You don't live that far from Zurina . . . I guess I could walk and be there in about an hour."

There was a long pause between us. I didn't know what his pause meant, but mine was filled with thoughts of him offering to pay for a cab—very much like the night he offered up his Green Bay Packers jacket. After what seemed like a minute I broke the silence by telling him I was on my way.

I don't know why I told him I would be there in an hour. I wasn't even ready to go. I frantically moved through Zurina's house going through my clothes. I had meticulously selected my outfit for our "date" but as I looked at the clothes I packed to the brim of my bookbag, nothing appealed to me. Although Zurina and I had barely exchanged words since our fight earlier, my only other option was to borrow something from her.

"Zurina, I know you are pissed off at me right now, but I was hoping that you would let me borrow something to wear."

"Go ahead–just be careful not to get anything on them."

"Thank you, thank you, thank you, you are the best friend any girl could ever ask for."

I went in for a hug, but before I could get within a foot of her she turned away from me. Prior to her turning I caught a glimpse of the disappointment in her eyes. She knew there was nothing she could say to me to change my mind. I didn't like that we were fighting. She already had so much on her mind related to her mom and I selfishly added to her stress with my desire to be with someone who probably didn't really give a damn about me. For a second I wondered if I should call the whole thing off. That thought left me quickly as I imagined being with Max.

Dressed and ready to go I left the apartment building for Drake Road. I have to admit I was a little nervous about walking outside alone at night. Although I had done it many times before, the fear of something bad happening to me remained for my hour-long trek. By the time I got to Max's it was 11:30 p.m.

Max's dad came to the door and called for him and Max indicated that I could come up to his bedroom. The house was completely dark except for the light from the television and Max's room. When I stepped inside, the thought of being in Max's house and just the two of us in his bedroom overwhelmed me. The front porch was the closest I had come to being inside and that was during the day. The graveyard across the street was the closest I had come at night.

I was taken back when I started to long for that graveyard. Even though I heard horror stories about graveyards, I preferred being there over being inside this dark house. This was especially true when I encountered the dog that had to be held back by Max's father as I carefully walked past it to get to the stairs.

When I reached the top of the stairs, I caught wind of Nate, Max's brother, and his friend Rodolfo whom I went to middle school with. We awkwardly exchanged hellos, and as I walked into Max's room, I heard them chuckling. I wondered what they were laughing about but when I heard Max's voice my only thought was him. He was sitting on his bed rolling a blunt when I entered the room and didn't bother to look up at me until he was done.

"Girl, what took you so long?"

"I underestimated how long it was going to take me to walk here. Sorry."

"It's cool. I don't have anything going on tonight. I was just waiting

47

on you. Close that door."

He lit up the blunt and then walked over to the window to open it.

"My dad is usually cool with most anything I do, but he hates the smell of weed."

I caught a glimpse of the graveyard through the trees and it took me right back to the night where Max had been so thoughtful.

"Hey girl, you want to hit this? You alright?'

"Yes. Why do you ask?"

"Because I've been trying to get your attention. You must have been in a daze. What's on your mind?"

"Nothing. I'm good."

"You didn't answer my question. Do you want to hit this or not? You seem stressed. It will help you relax."

"I'm good, but thank you."

I dared not tell him I was thinking about the night in the graveyard. He would have surely thought I was pathetic.

I had witnessed so many of my friends get high. The laughter, the munchies, the ease, the paranoia. None of that appealed to me. Plus I felt the need to stay alert. I was already in this vulnerable position. Smoking would only heighten the paranoia that I felt right now, and that wouldn't do me much good. I wanted to appear in control.

When Max got done smoking he turned on Dr. Dre's *The Chronic*. While *Nothing But a "G" Thang* blasted on the boombox, Max asked me to sit close to him. I giggled, but complied without hesitation.

"I'm glad you came over. You know I've been curious about you for a while now. Ever since I first met you, I felt a connection. What about you?"

"Yes. I liked you instantly."

"Me too. What I want to know at this moment is what it feels like to kiss you. Can I kiss you?"

Before I could respond, he stared directly in my eyes for a few seconds before he leaned in and kissed me. I became hot all over and after a few seconds I pulled away.

"What's wrong?"

"Nothing, I just . . . "

"You just what?"

"I just don't know about this, about us."

"What about us?"

"I'm afraid, that's all. I heard about you. You've been with a lot of girls. I don't want to be like them."

"You're not going to be like them. I don't know what you heard about me. Yes, I've been with quite a few people, but you're different."

"How so?"

"They never meant anything to me. I didn't feel for them what I feel for you. This feeling is different. I like you. I could see us together."

"You could?"

"Yes, so can we get back to finishing that kiss?"

Once again, I didn't respond, which was an indication to Max that we could. This time when he kissed me, I didn't resist. After several minutes of making out, he abruptly stopped and got up to turn off the lights. When he returned we began kissing again, but this time the weight of his body pulled us to a lying position on the bed. And then the phone rang.

"Hey man, what's up?"

"Nothing much."

"I'm in for the night."

"No man, I told you, I'm in for the night."

"Yeah, I do."

"Naw man, how many times do I have to tell you that I'm chilling!"

"Fuck, you're annoying as shit. I'm hanging up now."

"No. I'm good. I'm busy."

"Because it's none of your business."

"No. Don't. I already have plans."

"Hello, hello, hello."

The line must have gone dead, because Max hung up the phone without saying bye. I couldn't hear anything the person he was talking to was saying. Max approached me again to continue where we left off, but before he could kiss me again, I asked about who was on the phone.

"Who was that?"

"No one."

"That didn't sound like no one."

"Dave."

"Who's Dave?"

"You remember him. He was over here a few weeks ago. Remember when we were all standing outside in my front yard?"

"Oh yeah. I remember him now. What did he want?"

"He wanted me to hang out. This dude won't take no for an answer."

"Sounded like it. Is he on his way over?"

"That's what he said, but he's just talking shit to try to get me to go hang with him."

"Maybe I should go."

"No, stay."

So I did. We commenced to kiss again, which evolved into me laying on top of him and then him laying on top of me. His hand went up my shirt and cupped my left breast. I forced him to move his hand repeatedly until we were interrupted by headlights. Max got off the bed and went to the window to see who it was. I sat on the bed and waited in dark silence.

"Damn, I told this dude I wasn't going anywhere tonight." Max scurried to turn on his light and looked at me apologetically. "Don't worry. I'll get them to leave."

"It's cool. He can stay if that's what you want. "

I didn't mean it but wanted to seem cool–like I was being supportive of his friend although I was deeply uncomfortable.

I stood up and asked where the bathroom was. In the bathroom I gathered myself as much as I could although my hair was now a mess and my clothes were wrinkled as if they had been sitting in the dryer for days. While in the bathroom I felt a surge of panic, but told myself that I had nothing to worry about while taking deep breaths. I then overheard Max and Dave talking.

"Man, I told you not to show up at my house like this. I'm busy."

"You just have some chick here. It's cool. I won't be here for long."

"No man, you should go. For real. This isn't cool. Plus why the fuck did you bring a gang of folks here? Tonight is different, man. You aren't going to convince me to come out."

"Take a chill pill. I said we'd only be here for a minute. You said you weren't coming out. That doesn't mean we can't bring the party to you."

"But see, that's the thing. I'm not in a partying kind of mood, so y'all are going to have to get the fuck out of here."

"Man, she's just some hoe. What happened to bros before hoes? You are on some other kind of shit tonight."

"Damn, man. She's not a hoe, you don't even know her. But it's cool, you can stay for a minute. You are fucking relentless."

After overhearing the exchange between Drew and Max, not to mention the many other male voices that filled the space, I didn't want to leave the bathroom. I had no idea how I was going to get myself out of this situation so I paced the bathroom and then plopped down on the toilet when I couldn't conjure up anything. I attempted to take some deep breaths but quickly stopped. There was no form of deep breathing in the world that was going to comfort me. I had to get myself together before I came out of the bathroom. I didn't want to seem rattled by the thoughts that were racing through my mind. I had no idea how many people were on the other side of the bathroom door. I was definitely going to leave now. I took one last glance in the mirror and walked out of the bathroom.

"Hey," was all I could muster when I entered Max's room. And then, "Max, I'm going to take off now."

"Don't go, we just got here. Why are you in a rush to leave?" Dave asked.

I lied, "I was actually planning to leave right before you guys got here. It has nothing to do with you."

"That's not the impression I got when I was talking to Max. It was my understanding you'd be here for a while." he retorted with a sly look on his face.

His words were vexing. I overheard every word Max said and he never even told Dave I was with him. I couldn't understand why he was making it seem like he knew what Max and I had been up to before he arrived. When I looked up and saw all eyes on me, it made me want to disappear. I had never been comfortable with being the center of attention and now I was in a room with six boys whose eyes were fixated on me. Heat rushed through my body which I hoped didn't show on my face. When I finally opened my mouth my voice cracked.

"As I said before, I was just leaving. Max, can you pass me my purse?"

Max started looking around for my purse, but stopped when Dave chimed in, "No. We'll leave, hold up a second. Let me talk to Max. Can we get some privacy? Go in the room next door."

I didn't like the way that Dave barked commands at me, but instead of giving that any attention, I looked at Max to see what he wanted me to do. He nodded, which was my cue to go to the guest room. Max followed me out, opened the door to the other room, and said it shouldn't be long and closed the door behind him.

I put my ear to the wall to try and hear what they were saying, but no matter how hard I tried I couldn't because they were whispering. I wondered what was being said, but they would be gone soon, so it honestly didn't matter. I sat back on the bed and a few minutes later, Max and Dave came into the room. I wasn't expecting both of them. I instantly felt something was gravely wrong so I stood up, but Dave urged me to sit back down. I obliged.

"We were thinking that we could all have a little fun tonight," said Dave.

"What do you mean by fun?"

"Well, we were thinking we could all do you."

"I'm not sure what you mean."

"I mean, that we could all fuck you."

I laughed, "You're joking, right?!?!?"

"I've been known to joke about a lot of things, but I'm definitely not joking about this."

"Well the answer is no."

"Think about it. You might like it."

"I'm sure I wouldn't like it. It's really time for me to go now."

I stood up to leave but he shoved me back on the bed. I looked at Max and his eyes were locked on me but no words were coming out of his mouth.

"Max, what the fuck is going on? This isn't right, just let me go home. I'm not okay with this."

Max continued to stare at me for a while and then said with a coldness I had never heard from him, *"You have five minutes to decide."*

"Okay, the joke is over Max. Ha ha, this isn't funny."

"It was never meant to be funny. Demarra, this isn't a game. Like I said, five minutes. Make a decision so we don't have to make one for you."

"My decision is made. I told you no. That is my decision, goddamn it. Now I'm leaving for real."

I got up to leave but this time Max pushed me back down on the bed.

"No, Max, please don't do this to me. Please just let me go home."

Max gets up to leave and says, *"Like I said, five minutes."* Dave follows and closes the door behind him.

I look at the clock. 12:35 a.m. I get up from the bed. I'm pacing now. I look at the window and try to decide if I can get out of the room that way. I'm afraid of breaking an arm, a leg. And then I think that I could leave the room and run down the stairs. But the thought of the dog stops me in my tracks. Then I consider screaming. I didn't know his dad. I didn't know if he would protect me–if he would even care. I decided against anything that could potentially make matters worse. Maybe they wouldn't really try to hurt me. Maybe they were playing a sick joke on me. Maybe they would come in and we would have a good laugh about all this. It's 12:37 now.

If this was real, what could I say to get myself out of it? My thoughts were too jumbled to come up with anything. 12:40 on the dot. The doorknob turns, Max enters and Dave files in behind him. My eyes meet Max's, hoping he will take pity on me. Instead he says, *"Times up, what is it going to be?"*

"I already told you. I haven't changed my mind. I'm still thinking you guys are just trying to scare me. Okay, it worked. Now can I go home?"

Dave pulls out a gun, sits down on the armchair adjacent to the bed, lies the gun on his lap and says, "Why do you have to make this so hard? You know you want to. Why else would you be here late at night with Max?"

"Max is one thing. I liked Max. I thought he liked me too. I would have never come if I knew all of you were going to end up coming over."

"It's too late. We're all here now and we're not leaving until we get something from you."

"I don't plan to give you what you want so just let me go home."

"Let me see if I can make this simple for you." he says as he gets up from the chair and walks towards me. He hovered over me and placed the gun on my right temple. "Either you give us what we want or we're going to have a problem."

I had never seen a gun before in real life. I started crying and pleading, but it was no use. It was decided. They would have their way with me.

Dave commands me to get off the bed and go into the other room. Max opens the door as I move towards it, tears flowing, with my eyes locked on the floor. I look up once to make eye contact with Max. He keeps his eyes on mine as I slowly walk out the room, but doesn't utter a word. As soon as we lose eye contact, I look back down at the floor.

Once inside the room, voices are ordering me to take off my clothes, but the only voice I recognize is Dave's. He threatens that if I do not comply they will hurt me. He pulls out the gun again and places it on my left temple this time and tells me to hurry the fuck up. And follows with, "Shut up or I just might pull the trigger." The crying never stopped.

"Shut up, bitch," he said. "You are pathetic to look at. I don't even know if this bitch will be worth it. Hurry up. Take off your damn clothes so we can get this shit over with."

I complied but I barely had any energy. I wasn't sure if it was all the crying I had done or the mental and emotional exhaustion, but I felt as if I was moving in slow motion.

"You are the slowest goddamn girl in all of history. Damn, bitch, I'm not going to keep repeating myself. Hurry the fuck up," barked Dave. Then the others chimed in.

"Yeah, this bitch couldn't be any slower if she tried."

"Look at her; boo, the fuck, hoo."

"Man, doesn't she look weak."

"This shit is hilarious yo, I can't wait to tell everyone I know about this."

What was about to happen was unbearable, but the thought of other people knowing was that much more painful to consider. My mind started to drift to the past. Being at the beach with my family on the fourth of July, riding my bike, playing basketball, football, soccer, tag, walking around my neighborhood. Anything that had ever brought me joy flashed through my mind until there was nothing left. A blank slate. And then I was drifting, lucid, as light as a feather.

Completely naked I got in bed and Max, Dave, and Dave's four friends, one by one did what they wanted to me, while Rodolfo & Nate watched in amusement, chuckling every so often. Hearing them laugh at me was like a knife cutting through my skin.

I lay there with my gaze on a spot on the wall and then an image of myself staring down at me appeared. We seemed to be looking past each other, with our eyes never meeting. My focus went from the spot and the image of myself repeatedly until it was over. And then the image was gone. We rejoined but now we were altogether different.

It took me immense strength to remove myself from the bed and put on my clothes. I did so in silence and then commenced to leave as quickly as possible. On my way out of Max's room, my eyes stayed cast on the floor. I was too ashamed to look up at anyone. Dave and his friends bantered with a sense of pride that made me ill. Max seemed disinterested in this and instead blocked me at the door. I stood in front of him for a while before I asked him to please move while keeping my head hung low. When he didn't move, my eyes moved from the floor to his eyes, and I let out a voice that didn't seem like my own.

"Can you please get the fuck out my way?"

He didn't respond to my question, and instead grabbed my arm with gentleness that sent jolts through my body. I pulled away as quickly as I could, but he continued to block my escape route, and said, *"Demarra, let me call you a cab."*

It was as if nothing had happened. Like we were back in the cemetery again, except we weren't. Max, the guy that I had been head over heels crazy about raped me. He allowed his friend to rape me. He allowed Nate and Rodolfo to be entertained by my suffering. Everyone was despicable for what they had done to me, but Max was the most despicable of them all.

"I don't need anything from you. Please don't ever contact me again. Please get out of my way so I can go home. I just want to go home."

"You don't mean that. I'll call you later today to check on you. Are you sure I can't get you a cab?"

There was a hint of sadness in his voice. I loathed him, but for whatever reason, I also took pity on him. Nevertheless, I looked him square in the eyes this time before I responded.

"Dude, you can't be serious after what just happened. I hate you. I will always hate you. Never call me again and get the fuck out of my way so I can get out of this hell hole."

Dave chimed in, "Man, you're gonna let this bitch talk to you like that? I'd be careful if I were you. That's a long walk home. You wouldn't want to find yourself in a ditch before you made it there."

Max didn't respond, but he finally moved out of the way. I walked past him and down the stairs as quickly as I could before storming out the door. I never looked back, but I assumed the steps that followed were Max's.

My heart raced as I walked outside in the cold air. I was too weak to walk all the way back to Zurina's, plus I was petrified that Dave would follow me. After hearing his words about me being in a ditch, and after what he had just done to me, I couldn't predict if he was serious. I walked to the end of Max's driveway and decided I would take a right to throw them off in case they had indeed planned to come after me.

The strength I had just a few minutes before when confronting Max waned. Flashes of me getting undressed, lying in Max's bed naked, eight sets of eyes watching me, overtook my emotions. I only made it about a block before I broke down to the ground and began to cry.

Once I calmed myself down, I realized I still didn't know where I was going. And then I remembered that Tessa lived close by. We had only hung out a few times before, but she was my only other option. I moved as quickly as I could, but my crying, at times, was so potent that it stopped me dead in my tracks.

When I finally made it to Tessa's house, I just stood on the sidewalk and stared at her front door with a ton of questions flashing through my mind.

What would she think of me?

Who would come to the door?

Was she even home?

Would her mom forbid her to see me after this?

As much as I feared how Tessa and her mom would respond to me, I didn't have it in me to walk anymore and it was too cold to sleep outside. I rang Tessa's doorbell a few times, trying hard to gain my composure before someone came to the door. When Tessa's mom answered I mustered every bit of energy I had to try to hold back the tears. I opened my mouth but there was no sound. All I had were tears that seemed to be endless. Ms. Jacobs just looked at me, stunned, and then she took me in her arms and just held me which made me cry even more.

She managed to get me through the front door and reassured me that it would be okay. I didn't feel like it was ever going to be okay. How could it? My world as I knew it had shattered.

She then told me to have a seat in the living room, and that she'd go and wake Tessa.I sat there in darkness while I waited for her. For the first time in my life the darkness scared me. The silence scared me too.

When Tessa entered the room, I was too ashamed to look at her for more than a brief moment and then went into another intense crying spell. Tessa immediately hugged me tightly, and the tears flowed even more rapidly now. Neither Tessa or her mom asked me any questions. They just simply let me cry myself to sleep. For the remainder of the night I came in and out of crying and sleeping. And this is how it was for the days that followed.

TRAUMA'S AFTERMATH

Chapter 5
Please Believe Me

The next morning I awoke at Tessa's and all I felt was hollow. Tessa's mom insisted on calling my mother but I begged her not to. I didn't want to suffer any more than I had and I knew she would be infuriated about me sneaking out. Plus I would have to explain what happened and I wasn't ready to do that. I didn't even want to admit it to myself.

When I finally got enough courage to begin talking, hours after Tessa and her mom drove me home, I started with my friend Jahzara. She tried to be supportive but the tone of her voice and the way she questioned me made me feel like she didn't believe me.

Then I called Zurina. The moment she picked up the phone I could tell she was still angry with me. I cast that aside, pretending that the tension wasn't there and continued to talk to her like I always had, except this time it was to tell her the horrific details of what happened. I spoke quickly, barely breathing between what should have been natural pauses. Once I told her every detail I could remember I stopped talking, and there was nothing but silence.

"Zurina, are you still there?"

"Yes, I'm here."

"So you don't have anything to say to what I just said to you?"

"No, I don't."

"I just told you I was raped, and this is your response?"

"Yes, Demarra, I told you not to go over there. What did you expect would happen?"

"Definitely, not this. What are you saying?"

"I'm saying that by going to Max's after I urged you not to, it's on you."

"I'm so confused. What do you mean it's on me?"

"I mean you brought this on yourself."

I couldn't believe what I was hearing. All this time I thought Zurina was my friend, my best friend to be exact. We did everything together, had seen the intricate details of each other's lives, bonded over the broken relationships we had with our mothers. In an instant, everything I felt for her vanished. I had never felt so broken. Not only had this unthinkable thing just happened to me, but the closest friend I had was turning her back on me when I needed her the most. I had to end the conversation before I broke into tears. I didn't have the strength to fight that battle, and it was clear my tears weren't safe here.

"Thank you for listening. I'll be okay. I'm not the first or last person to go through something like this. Tomorrow will be better."

"No problem. You know I love you."

"Sure. Talk to you later."

I knew tomorrow wouldn't be better. I knew that I wouldn't be better. I desperately wanted that though. This abyss that settled in my body was unbearable.

For the remainder of the weekend, I stayed in my room with the door closed. I didn't eat, it was hard to sleep, and my thoughts were consumed with flashbacks of that night. Neither Jahzara or Zurina checked on me all weekend.

Monday morning I got out of bed to get ready for school. I practiced smiling in the mirror several times in an attempt to make it seem like everything was fine. As soon as I got to school, I instantly noticed that nearly every group of students I passed was whispering about me as evidenced by their stares, points, and snickers. Many of these students I had gone to school with for years; some of them I thought were my friends. This continued between classes and then at lunch I discovered that Rodolfo and Nate started a rumor that I participated willingly in a gang bang. It was hard enough to concentrate when I kept replaying over and over again what happened, but now I had become a social pariah for something that wasn't even true.

I desperately wanted to disappear. Everyone's eyes were on me and the whispers were everywhere. The final bell of the day rang and I walked to my locker as quickly as I could, looking down nearly the entire time for fear of making eye contact with anyone. When I turned down the hall where my locker was, I noticed Rodolfo and Nate leaning up against a wall directly across from my locker. This made no sense to me considering their lockers weren't in this part of the school. I continued to look down as I got my things. They started to taunt me with their laughter, just as they did the night of the rape. But now they were spouting lies about me and making it seem that I was promiscuous, loose, easy.

I ignored them, gathered my things as quickly as possible, and walked with enormous speed to get on the bus to go home. Instead of sitting with Zurina I sat alone. I looked out the window and the tears started to flow.

Once home, I went straight to my room and got in bed. The four walls seemed to close in on me, and I increasingly found it difficult to breathe. I couldn't bare to live with the pain of my rape and rejection, not just from my peers, but also from the people who I thought cared about me. I had to make it stop.

I got up from my bed and headed towards the bathroom. I opened the medicine cabinet, scanning each bottle before landing on Ibuprofen. I opened the bottle and emptied all the pills in the palm of my hand–24 to be exact. I put the pills in my pocket, placed the empty bottle back in the cabinet, and went to the kitchen to pour myself a glass of water before heading back to my room and locking my door. I swallowed the first five pills one by one and then put the remaining small reddish orange pills in my mouth and swallowed them all in one gulp. I turned off the lights, got in bed, pulled the covers over my head, and told myself it would all be over soon.

I awoke in a hospital bed surrounded by people I didn't know, with my mother by my side, as my stomach was being pumped.

"Where am I?"

"Borgess Hospital."

"What happened? Who brought me here?"

"You don't know how you got here?"

"No, that is what I just said."

"So you don't know what you were doing prior to coming here today?"

"The last thing I remember is . . ."

"Is what?"

"Well, I was laying down in my bed."

"Do you remember anything else?"

"I took some pills."

"So, you took the pills willingly?"

"Yes."

"Why?"

"I'm assuming you already know the answer to that question."

"We want to hear from you. We have thoughts about why you did it, but we don't want to assume anything."

"I don't really want to talk about it."

"Since you aren't in the talking mood, we will tell you why we think you did it. Is that okay?"

"Do I really have a choice in the matter?"

"There are always choices, but since you won't willingly tell us what happened, we need to help you tell your story."

I just looked at the medical staff. I didn't know how to respond. But what I did know was that regardless of what I had to say they already made up their mind about why I did what I did, and I'd be going to the Adolescent Psychiatric Unit as a result. I didn't want to carry that burden so I told them everything under the condition that my mother wouldn't be present. After I was done, I was escorted up to the Adolescent Psychiatric Unit, just as I suspected.

The next day I woke up on a plastic mattress nestled in a sand colored plywood frame. I felt like I had slept for days.

My most constant thought was Max. I still couldn't quite wrap my mind around the idea that the guy I thought could end up being my boyfriend had raped me. It felt surreal. Like I was in this constant state of dreaming. Although it had only been a few days since the incident, it felt like it had just happened. I wanted answers so I made up my mind that I would call him.

Although it wasn't free reign for us to use the phone except for matters concerning contacting our parents or whomever was taking care of us, we were allowed to make outside calls to others during certain times of the day. For these types of calls we could use a pay phone that was right across from the nurses station.

I rolled out of bed and noticed that the bed next to mine was perfectly made. In fact every inch of that side of the room was tidy. This intrigued me. I had always been so messy. I usually knew where to find the things I needed although if anyone saw my room they would wonder how that was even possible. My roommate was nowhere in sight but I looked forward to meeting her, and desperately hoped that we would get along. And then there was a knock at the door.

"Yes."

"Demarra, this is Dr. Anand. I wanted to check in with you to see how your morning is going."

"I'm not quite dressed yet, can you please come back in a few minutes?"

"Actually, I can't. I have other patients to see. Please hurry up and get dressed. I'll give you one minute. Will that be enough time?" I knew I really didn't have a choice in the matter. I hated when adults did that. They had every intention of doing what they wanted, so why they took the time to inquire with us was perplexing.

"I guess."

After what didn't even seem like a whole minute had passed, Dr. Anand knocked again.

"Demarra, I'm coming in now so please confirm you're dressed."

"Yes I am. You may come in."

Once he walked in I attempted to size him up instantly. By the looks of him and his accent I assumed he was of Indian descent. He was tall, had dark hair, wore black rimmed glasses, and a white jacket with a pen inside the pocket that made him seem like he would be more suitable in a lab. I also noticed he was carrying a clipboard.

"May I sit down?"

"Sure."

"Demarra, as I said before my name is Dr. Anand. I am the psychiatrist on duty here at the Borgess Adolescent Psychiatric Unit."

"Okay."

"How are you feeling today?"

"Fine, I guess."

"When you say fine can you try to replace that word with a feeling?"

"I feel fine."

"So is that happy, sad, melancholy?"

"What is that?"

"You mean melancholy?"

"Yes."

"I guess the best way to describe it is not happy or sad, but maybe in the middle of those two feelings. Or maybe not all the way sad, but a little sad."

"Oh."

"So again, how do you feel?"

"I already told you—fine."

"Yes you did, but what I am looking for is an actual feeling word."

I just stared directly in his eyes silently. I could tell this made him feel uncomfortable because he looked away.

"Do you think you might need help identifying what you feel?"

"No, I don't need help."

"Well then, tell me how you feel."

"I already told you."

"No, you said you were fine. Fine is not a feeling. Although you said you don't need help identifying what you feel, your inability to tell me what you feel makes me think you need help."

"Look, I already told you I don't need help. I am starting to get agitated by our interaction and your presence in my room. I'm sure you have already read my chart and know the terrible things that happened to me so the fact that you are asking me how I am doing, how I am feeling, is puzzling to me."

"What is puzzling to you about it? And I am unsure as to why you are having these strong feelings. All I am asking you to do is tell me how you feel."

"Look, Dr. whatever . . . "

"Anand."

"What?"

"My name is Dr. Anand."

"Okay, Dr. Anand, as I was saying. You've read my chart. You should already know how I feel right now."

"How am I supposed to know what you are feeling if you don't tell me what you are feeling?"

"You must have a sense of what I'm feeling. How long have you been doing this? I'm sure you've seen patients in my condition before. Isn't that what this place is for? Teenagers like myself who are fucked-up in the head? Who have had pretty fucked-up shit happen to them?"

"Yes, you're right. I can imagine what you might feel, but that wouldn't be fair for me to tell you what I think you feel considering I am not you. I haven't experienced what you've experienced. Based on everything you just said and the manner in which you said it I think you are angry. Is that correct?"

"Sure. You could say that."

"Okay, are you feeling anything else?"

"I don't know what to feel."

"That's understandable. What about thoughts of taking your life? Are you having any thoughts like that?"

"No."

"Okay. Do you agree to talk to someone on staff if you begin to have those feelings?"

"Sure."

"This is very important. It is everyone's job to keep you safe while you're here."

"Yes. Got it."

Then Dr. Anand got up to leave. On his way out he shared he would plan on seeing me tomorrow for another check-in which I wasn't looking forward to. And then he asked if I planned to join the others for breakfast.

I wasn't hungry, but I was eager to meet the other people in the hospital. Breakfast happened in the community room, which was also the place we played games and watched television. Although the decor was old and the artwork was similar to what you'd see at a hospital, there were also motivational messages, much like I saw in school, on the stark off-white walls that I guess were there to aid us in our treatment. As I looked at these messages, like, *"Excellence," "Make It Happen," "Teamwork," and "Believe & Succeed,"* I was amused. I didn't feel any of these things about myself anymore and the way my friends had turned on me in the midst of experiencing so much pain made me deeply skeptical of teamwork.

All I could manage to eat was a sparse amount of raisin bran with skim milk and a small glass of orange juice. I had a craving for a cigarette which I knew wasn't going to happen anytime soon. This made me feel agitated. I told myself I had better try to make the best of my situation since I didn't know how long I was going to be at the hospital, and I really didn't feel like being on restriction. In the midst of that thought, I looked up because I had a feeling someone was staring at me. My eyes met with a boy I quickly discovered was James. He had this grin on his face that made me feel slightly uncomfortable. I quickly looked away. The thought of males, period, disgusted me, but there was something kind about his eyes.

After breakfast it was time for group therapy which was separated by gender. Initially I didn't understand why we separated based on our gender but then I realized that I wouldn't feel comfortable talking about my problems, especially involving my rape, around males. So this actually made me relieved. Honestly, I didn't know if I felt comfortable talking about my issues at all. But I wanted to get out of this place as quickly as possible and the only way I could do that was by contributing in a way that would at least make it seem like I was stable enough to leave.

We started Group by taking turns stating our name and sharing what we felt. Even if you didn't feel like talking, you would have to participate. I watched each person closely as they shared. I was particularly interested when a girl named Miley spoke. I could tell she was one of those white girls that had spent a lot of time with Black people, and perhaps hoped she was Black because of the way she spoke and how she dressed. I was so stuck on how she was talking that I didn't pay attention to the words that were coming out of her mouth. I did notice that her eyes kept reverting to me while she was talking, though. I wondered if it was because she felt I was looking through her and not at her. Nevertheless, it didn't make me uncomfortable enough to make me stop. When it was my turn, although I hadn't intended to, I just started sharing what brought me to the hospital, as if someone else was in control of my vocal cords. All eyes were on me which made sense because I was sharing, but I didn't know if it was in pity, disbelief, or both. 'Thanks for sharing your truth," spouted by all at the end provided me no insight on this. When Group was over, Miley approached me in the hall and asked if we could talk.

"Sure. What do you want to talk about?"

"Well, I would prefer to talk in private. Do you mind if we chat during down-time?"

"Okay."

"Cool. I'll come to your room. Do you think your roommate will be there?"

"I'm not sure. I haven't actually seen her all morning."

"Do you think you could check? What I have to talk to you about is private."

"Private? That's a little weird since we just met. I'm starting to feel like maybe we shouldn't."

"It's not like that. There was something you said in group that I wanted to talk to you about. I just figured that us girls speaking in private would probably be more comfortable for us both."

"Oh, okay. I get it. Yeah. I'll check and let you know."

I found out the reason I hadn't seen my roommate was because she had been placed on restriction and wouldn't be back for a while. The staff wouldn't give me any details but it didn't take a rocket scientist to figure out what it meant–she was on suicide watch. I didn't like the idea of being in the room by myself but decided not to put any energy into it considering there was nothing I could do about it. I went and found Miley and she followed me to my room.

She sat down at the desk and I sat on my bed. Facing me now she just stared at me for a long time before I broke the silence.

"What's going on? Why are you looking at me like that?"

"I'm just trying to figure you out."

"What do you mean you're trying to figure me out?"

"I'm just trying to determine why you would lie about my boyfriend."

"I don't know what the hell you're talking about."

"I'm talking about you saying that my boyfriend raped you."

I was startled and offended by her accusations. I had no idea who her boyfriend was. I named each of my attackers during Group. One of them must have been her boyfriend.

"Who is your boyfriend?"

"Demetrius."

"Oh. So what are you asking me?"

"I'm asking why you would lie about him raping you."

"I'm not lying. Why would I lie about something like that?"

"I don't know, shit. I don't know you. You could be lying. I mean, hell, people lie all the time about all types of shit. Who knows why they do it. I just know there is no way he could do something like that. We've been dating for months. I would know if he were capable of something like that."

I just looked at her. I didn't know what good defending myself would be. Plus I didn't feel like it was my job to convince her. She could feel whatever she wanted to feel. I had been down this road before with people who I knew, loved, and yet didn't believe me, so there was no way I would be able to convince her. Instead I just sat in silence until Miley broke it.

"So you aren't going to change your story?"

"No, I'm not. Why would I? It happened."

"So if it happened, then tell me everything starting with how he looked."

"You really want me to do that?"

"Yes I do. Convince me that I'm wrong about you."

"I don't need to convince you of anything."

"True dat. Well this is my boyfriend we're talking about here. I just want to know if he really did it. I'm not interested in going out with someone who may be a rapist. On the other hand, this is the first time I met you. I've never even heard of you before now. You could be one of those girls, you know . . ."

"No. I don't know."

"Sure you do. You know like one of those chicks who sleep with anybody and everybody and then all of a sudden when people find out they wanna call rape."

"I understand."

"So are you going to divulge or not? We only have like thirty minutes left of free time so if you plan on telling you should probably start now."

"I feel like I already did, in Group. I don't have the energy. Either you believe me or you don't. That's up to you."

When Miley realized I wasn't going to tell her what she wanted, she simply got up and left my room, and we barely spoke after that.

I woke up the next day to find that my roommate had still not returned. I felt much hungrier than the day before so I quickly got myself together so I could have breakfast. As I was finishing my last bite, I looked up to a voice asking me if the seat next to mine was taken. It was James. I quickly told him no it wasn't and that he could sit there if he liked. Before I completed my sentence he was already sitting down. After I was finished I got up to throw my stuff away.

"Why are you in such a rush? If I was paranoid I would think you were avoiding talking to me."

"Why would you say that? As you can see I'm finished with my breakfast."

"I can see that. Why don't you stay and chat for a while? Unless, of course, you have something better to do."

Although his sarcasm was slightly annoying, he was right. I was going to go back to my room, but there it would just be me, my thoughts, and the silence. I decided I would avoid all that for now and stay and talk to James, but I didn't want to give in to him so I was coy instead.

"I actually do have something better to do. I was planning to go back to my room to get ready for the day."

"Well we have a whole two hours until Group so I'm pretty sure you have time."

"Why would you assume something like that? You don't know how long it takes me to get ready."

"I'll give you that one. But from watching you since yesterday, you seem like you're pretty low key. Not like other girls who take forever to get ready. I don't even think you wear makeup and unless you're going to do something different with your hair than wear it in a bun, I would guess it takes you about twenty minutes to get ready–shower and all."

"You think you're so smart, don't you?"

"As a matter of fact I am. Don't take me the wrong way though. I'm not trying to be a smart ass. I'm just trying to convince you to stay and chat for a while. You seem like someone I would enjoy getting to know."

I didn't know what to say in response to him. This dude was persistent. I knew I didn't really want to get involved with someone, but I had to admit I liked the attention.

"Okay. I guess you're right. I can stay for a little while."

I discovered that James was in the unit due to severe anger issues. He would lash out at any and every thing that he perceived to be a threat. One of the biggest threats involved himself. He had recently attempted to take his life, too. I didn't know if I should ask him why he felt that way. Although I didn't want to intrude, he seemed at ease with me so I decided I would probe.

"Why do you think you wanted to die?"

"Tired I guess."

"Of what?"

"You know . . . life in general."

"What's so bad about your life?"

"It sucks. It has sucked for as long as I can remember. I don't feel like anyone understands me, appreciates me. You know what I'm saying?"

"I guess so."

"My dad has been gone since I was born. My mom has had boyfriends in and out of my life for years. I have so much anger sometimes that I have to figure out a way to release it. Unfortunately, sometimes I turn against myself."

"I know what you mean."

"How could you possibly know what I mean? I don't know any girl who does some of the crazy shit I've done."

"How do you think I got in here? How do you think any of the girls who are here got here? We all did something crazy to get here. That is the nature of this place."

"Yeah, I know that, but girls are wired differently."

"Okay. What's your point? Just because we are wired differently doesn't mean we don't do similar things as guys."

"Like what?"

"I can only speak for myself. I can tell you I've gotten so angry that I attacked my brother and cousin with a butcher knife."

"Okay, okay. So we're both a little crazy, huh?"

We both laughed but deep down I didn't like the idea of not only someone thinking I was crazy, but owning that identity for myself.

"Anyway. The point is that emotions are the same for males and females. Although males may typically express their emotions differently than females, we all experience the same range of emotions. That's what makes us human."

"So, why are you here? Is it the knife incident?"

"No. It was something else. That is what brought me here last time."

"So this isn't your first time here? Maybe we are cut from the same cloth!"

"Oh, so this is your second time, too?"

"No, it is actually my third time. You would think that I had enough of this place."

"True."

"So what happened this time?"

"I'd rather not say."

"I just poured out my soul to you."

"You call that pouring out your soul? No offense, but I learned a few details about you relevant to why you are here. That doesn't equate to soul bearing."

"You're funny! So you're really not going to tell me?!?!"

"No. I don't really want to talk about it."

I looked up at the clock and saw that I only had thirty minutes until Group. The time had passed so quickly. I got up to leave in a rush so I could get ready. James grabbed my arm ever so gently and informed me that if I ever wanted to talk to someone he was eager to listen.

Back in my room I thought about how nice James was. I wondered how someone with all the anger he described could be so caring. That was the thing about human beings I was starting to discover—we are not always what we appear to be.

The thought of confronting Max entered my thoughts again. I wanted answers about what he did. I thought maybe he could explain something about the incident that would help me understand his reasoning for doing it. After all, I thought he liked me, cared about me. The thought of talking to Max consumed me during Group.

After Group I decided it was time to make that call. Although I didn't like the idea of not having any privacy, the desire to call Max superseded the concerns of others listening to my phone call. I put the quarter in the pay phone and dialed the number. After two rings he answered.

"Hello."

"Max?"

"Yeah. Who's this?"

"It's Demarra."

"Why the fuck are you calling me?"

"What do you mean why am I calling you? Because of what happened–what you did."

"I don't know what you're talking about."

"What do you mean you don't know what I'm talking about?"

"You heard what I said. Don't call me anymore. It's best if you lose my number–if you pretend you and I never met."

"Why? Because you feel guilty about what you did? How could you do that to me Max? I thought you liked me? How could you let this happen to me? How could you participate? Let your brother and his friend watch me? What kind of person does that?"

There was dead silence on the line. Tears were now rolling down my face heavily, uncontrollably. My breathing was exaggerated. I could feel my heart beating faster and my chest moving up and down like the beat of a drum.

"Max, answer me. Please answer me. I am just trying to make sense of all this. Please tell me what happened that night. What did I do to deserve it?"

"Demarra, whatever infatuation you had with me, hang it up. I don't like you. In fact, I never liked you. As I said before, lose my number. If you know what's good for you, you will keep your goddamn mouth shut and not discuss what you think happened that night. You're crazy and need help. Don't call me again!"

The phone went dead. I dropped to my knees and all I saw was blackness. I don't recall what happened the rest of the day or several days that followed. I do remember trying to call Max again later and hearing that the number had been disconnected. You would think hearing this message would deter me from calling again. It took twenty phone calls before it finally came to me. I would never have contact with Max again.

Today was visiting day. I had been in the hospital for one week and my treatment team felt I was now emotionally strong enough to have a family therapy session. Things had gotten so bad with my mom, however, I wasn't sure if repairing our relationship was possible, and I had very little connection to my father so there was that. Deep down I really wanted to see my family though. I loved them very much.

My mom showed up alone for the session. So did my father. I had always known my mother loathed my father. I remember getting in trouble when I was younger and my mother would tell me how I was going to be just like him. What I felt in those moments paled in comparison to what I felt when she told me he was one of the worst mistakes she had ever made. To me, those words signified she wished I had never been born; that my existence was also a mistake.

My father hadn't taken an active interest in my life, for the most part, until now, so to be compared to a man I barely knew anything about was perplexing. Although I had started spending time at his home over the last couple years, he never made time for me. He worked a lot and when he wasn't working he was out fishing, watching sports, or sleeping. I asked countless times about him taking me fishing with him, but he never did. The only times we spent time alone was when we went to the grocery store. Those rare opportunities of us riding in the car and walking through the aisles was something I hoped for when I'd visit for the weekend. He thought this made him a good father, along with the measly $50 a week he paid in child support. I didn't know if he realized how little $50 stretched when it involved taking care of another human being.

My father only started to consistently be in my life when my behavior became problematic for my mom. I felt ambivalent about him coming around for that reason. Although I wanted him in my life, I didn't only want him there in the midst of my problems, I longed for him to be in my life in every way. He had missed so many good things. I resented him for that. The time he was now trying to spend with me came a little too late in my opinion. Nevertheless, here we were in this room, with my therapist, to discuss my progress.

"Ms. Vause, Mr. Wade, thank you for coming in today. It is good to see you again. Are you ready to begin?" asked my therapist, Mr. Harring.

"No problem," said my father.

"Sure," replied my mother.

"And what about you, Demarra? Are you ready?"

"Yes. I'm ready."

"Wonderful. Before we get started I want to share that although this will be our first official family session, Demarra's progress will dictate how many additional sessions we have. While she is in treatment, however, I would like to schedule a minimum of one session per week until her discharge. Does that work for the two of you?"

"I work a lot. I will do my best to attend when I can," said my father.

"I see. Well your participation is very important related to Demarra's recovery."

"I understand that. Like I said, I will do my best. I have other children, much younger than Demarra, that I have to worry about, along with a wife."

I hated when he brought up his other children and his wife. He had been with them their whole lives, I on the other hand missed him for the majority of mine. Even these days, if I was lucky, I got to see him once a month.

My therapist must have realized that convincing my father to commit wasn't going to happen because then he swiftly moved on to my mother.

"What about you, Ms. Vause? Are you able to come to family sessions once per week?"

"Yes. I will do my best. I want to see my daughter get better. I also have other children, as you know, but as long as I know in advance I will make it a point to be here."

"What is that supposed to mean?" my father chimed in accusatorially.

"I mean that we all have obligations, but this is our child. She needs us both right now."

"I'm here, aren't I? Haven't I been here every time she has gotten in trouble over the last year?"

"You have, but where were you long before all this happened to her? Maybe if you had been here . . ."

"I am sorry to interrupt you, Ms. Vause, but might I remind us all that we are here to support Demarra. Although your feelings I'm sure are valid, we don't have time to hash it out right now. Time is precious for all of us. In looking at my watch we only have about forty minutes left for our session. Can we all agree to shift our focus to Demarra now?"

"Okay." my mother and father said begrudgingly.

"Great. So Demarra, let's start with you. Would you like to share how you are doing today and anything you might be feeling at the moment?"

"I'm feeling much better; I think I'm ready to go home."

"Home? Why do you think you're ready for home?"

"Because I have been participating fully in all aspects of my treatment program. I'm not having thoughts of hurting myself or others."

"All that you said is true, Demarra, but at this point we don't even know what caused you to try to hurt yourself in the first place. Plus, based on what I've read in your file there are serious issues at home involving your siblings. What do you feel, Ms. Vause, when you hear Demarra say she is ready to go home?"

"It concerns me. She has only been here for a week. There are a lot of unresolved issues we have. I'm not sure if having Demarra at home is what is best at this point."

"What do you mean it's not best. Then where would I go?" I barked.

"I haven't thought that far ahead. I'm just taking things one day at a time."

"You haven't thought about it? Well think about this! I'm locked up in here while everyone else is on the outside free."

"That is true, but sometimes when you're around we don't feel free. Do you know what it has been like worrying where you are at 2 a.m. or wondering if I'm going to get a call to come home from work because you and your brother or sister are fighting?"

"What about me? Why is it that I am always the one to blame for everyone else's problems? Why am I always the one cast aside? When will people listen to me, pay attention to what is going on with me?"

"Life has been hard for us all, Demarra. I have always done the best I can for you. I am at a loss. I don't know what more I can do to help you," said my mom.

"You can help me by getting me out of here. By allowing me to come home."

"I'm not saying you can never come home. Just not right now. You're not well."

"I'm fine."

"I wish that were true, but you're not fine. None of us are fine. We haven't been fine in a long time."

"And Mr. Wade, do you have anything you want to say to Demarra?"

"I love her. I haven't always been the best father, but I love my child. It hurts me to see her suffering this way."

"Do you mind looking at Demarra and saying that to her?"

"Demarra, I love you. Have always loved you. You know your middle name, that is a piece of me. I look at you and I see myself more in you than any of my other children. Please forgive me that I haven't always been there for you when you needed me. You know your dad has had some problems of his own over the years. Do you remember coming to see me in KPep? That was one of the happiest days of my life. You don't even know what I was in there for, do you?"

I shook my head indicating I didn't.

"It was for selling heroin. You know I was using too. I used it a lot actually. I have been clean ever since I got out of KPep. I'm trying to live my life on the straight and narrow. Working at Hexacomb has been good for me, but the money doesn't even compare to what I was making when I was hustling. I work a lot to try to compensate, not just for the fast money, but also for the time I lost with my family. I love you. I have always loved you. And I'm sorry."

His words moved me to tears. I wanted to believe every word that came out of his mouth, but he had hurt me so many times before. I was so tired of waiting for him to show up, waiting for him to get me that new item I wanted, waiting for him to make me a priority. I didn't want to wait any more.

"I love you too," is all I could manage to say.

"I feel like we are making progress today. Ms. Vause, I want to shift gears a little. I know you said that Demarra isn't ready to go home yet. What kinds of changes would you like to see before you would feel comfortable allowing her to come back home?"

"I need to see that Demarra can respond appropriately to rules and authority. She needs to be able to abide by a curfew and abstain from being around friends that aren't a good influence on her. I need to know that Demarra can deal with her emotions in a positive way. I can't be at work worrying if she is going to physically harm one of my other children. Not to mention that Demarra has the capacity to deal with her depression–if that is indeed what it is–without trying to take her life."

"Those seem like reasonable expectations. Demarra, what do you think?"

"I think I can continue working towards those things, but it can't just be me. Everyone has to be willing to do some work. I am not the only one in the family with the issues she just described, with the exception of the self-harm."

"And I need Demarra to take responsibility for her own actions. Hearing her say what she just said makes me think she is not being responsible for herself."

"No, mom. That is not the case at all. Didn't you hear what I said? I'm going to work on it. I just don't want to be the target of all the work. It's like you're in denial about everybody else's issues."

"I'm not in denial. I know good and well what is going on with your brothers and sister. Let me remind you that they are not the ones here. They are also not the ones who have done things that have forced them in a place like this now for the second time. And finally none of them have had the police at my home, on several occasions in the past, due to running away from home."

"See that is exactly what I'm talking about. Why do you have to bring all that old stuff up? Can't we just focus on today?"

"That is easy for you to say."

"Let me cut in please, Demarra. What your mother has described here today doesn't seem unreasonable. You indicated you were willing to put in the work to make the changes she desires, correct?"

"Yes."

"Okay, well let's start there. Can everyone agree on that?"

"Yes." we all said in unison.

"So, Demarra, related to the self-harm, are you ready to talk about what happened that caused you to want to hurt yourself?"

I looked around at everyone present. I wasn't ready. Not yet. I was still trying to convince myself it didn't happen. I wanted nothing more than to forget about the whole thing.

"No. I'm not ready to talk about it. I will say, however, that I won't attempt to hurt myself anymore. I haven't had one thought of suicide since I've been here."

"We won't push you to talk about it. Just know when you're ready we are here to listen. I do, however, want to explore how and why those feelings disappeared."

"I value my life. I've realized I want to live."

That was all I could think to say. It wasn't that I valued my life or even cared about myself, I just knew I didn't really want to die. I just wanted the pain to stop. I wanted the memories to be erased. I also wanted to get out of the hospital as soon as possible, so I would say damn near anything to make that a reality.

"I see. So when you say you value your life, you want to live, what does that mean exactly?"

"It means what I said. There is no underlying meaning."

"I understand. Since you're not able to articulate the meaning of what you described today, that will be your homework for our individual therapy session on Monday. You will write about why you value your life and why you want to live. Okay?"

Did I really have a choice in the matter? I knew anything they asked me to do would now become part of my treatment.

"Sure."

"Well, this ends our session. Let's plan for next Saturday at 2 p.m."

About two weeks after I was released from a five week stint at the hospital, my mom asked me why I took the pills. I wondered why after all this time she was asking me that. It had been a month and a half since the incident. I thought she knew. I thought they all knew in spite of the fact I was never willing to talk about it outside of Group.

"Demarra, it's okay. Whatever it is, you can tell me. I will do my best to understand."

"So you don't know what happened?"

"No."

"How is that possible?"

"I didn't inquire at the hospital about it. I was trying to allow you the space to tell me on your own. After all this time you haven't told me so I figured I would ask in hopes you would tell me."

I didn't know what to say. I was trying to move past this part of my life, but no matter how hard I tried, I simply couldn't. The story played in my mind over and over again like a broken record, but no one knew my thoughts so the story was safe there. I didn't know if I had it in me to tell the story again.

"Mom, I don't really want to . . . can't really . . . talk about it."

"Why not? Did someone hurt you?"

Those words rattled something inside me. I began crying much like I had the night of the attack. My mom consoled me. I would usually push her away, but not this time. I needed her arms of protection. I desperately wished I had it the night of the attack.

"Honey, whatever it is, we can get through it. I need to know what has happened. Maybe there is something I can do to help you."

"There is nothing you or anyone can do to help me mom. I am broken. What they did to me broke me. I am hollow. Do you know what it feels like to be hollow?"

"I do know that feeling. Dealing with some of the things I have had to deal with over the years has made me feel that way, too. I guess in some ways I still feel like that at times."

I wanted to tell her, but I was afraid that she, too, wouldn't believe me. And even if she did believe me, there was a possibility she would blame me. I had made the decision to go to Max's. I made out with him as we laid on his bed and he put his hand up my shirt. I knew I should have left as soon as Dave called. I didn't listen to my intuition when it told me to leave. I was ashamed that I had gone and I didn't even try to leave. I could have screamed. I could have fought but my fear overtook me that night. I did tell Max that I should leave, but he reassured me that everything would be okay. For some reason I trusted him when he told me that, so I went against everything my body was trying to tell me. That I was in the kind of danger that would nearly obliterate my existence. I just wish I had listened.

"I was raped," I blurted out.

"What did you just say?"

I knew she heard me, but was taken back by my words.

"Mom, I was raped."

"What do you mean you were raped?"

"I was raped. What do you mean, what do I mean?"

"I mean what happened? Who raped you?"

"There was a guy named Max that I liked. You know he called the house a few times. Well, while you were out of town I left Zurina's alone and walked to his house. It was supposed to be just the two of us. I had no intention of having sex with him. I just liked him a lot. I figured I would go over and we would just make out. Then his friend Dave called and informed him he would be coming over with some friends. I told Max I should leave. You know, I just didn't feel right about the whole thing. Max assured me that everything would be okay; that his friends were cool and they wouldn't be there that long. For some reason I trusted him so I went along with it. When they got there I instantly knew I had made a mistake. Being upstairs in Max's room alone with eight guys made me nervous. My stomach kept getting tighter and tighter, yet I stayed. When they propositioned me for sex I thought they were joking, but soon I realized they weren't. When I saw the gun I realized that I was in serious trouble, but it was too late. One by one, six of them raped me while two of them watched and laughed. When it was all over they threatened to kill me. I walked to Tessa's house because I was too weak to walk all the way back to Zurina's. They never did follow me."

"Honey, you have got to go to the police."

"Yes, mom I probably should, but I don't know what good it will do."

"It is worth a try. Those bastards shouldn't get away with what they did to you. Think about other girls. You wouldn't want that to happen to them, would you?"

"No, but he is in denial about the whole thing. Plus I think his dad has money so they could probably get a decent attorney."

"Okay, so what if they can get a good attorney? This is still worth fighting for, Demarra. What do you mean he is in denial? Have you spoken to him since the incident?

"Yes. I spoke to him once. He acted like he didn't know what I was talking about. He told me to forget we had ever met and for me to lose his number."

"That son of a bitch. We are pressing charges. I will take you down to file charges at the police station tomorrow."

It felt good to have her support. I didn't feel hopeful that anything would come of this, but it was worth putting in the effort to see how it would turn out. Just when I thought the conversation was over, she turned to me and said that I should never have gone.

The support I initially felt from her quickly turned to what I feared– that she would blame me for what happened. I don't think she intended to do that, but that's how it landed with me. I already knew I shouldn't have gone, but I really didn't need to hear that from her.

"Right, mom, goodnight," is all I could conjure up as I wiped my tears and headed up the stairs to my room.

The next day my mom and I headed to the police station together to file the report. When we arrived we were given a stack of papers and told to fill them out. Once the paperwork was complete we turned it into the officer and she told us that a detective would review the paperwork right away and then come and speak to us directly after if we had time to wait. My mom didn't have to be anywhere since she had taken the day off to do this with me. She also thought it would be best to stay in hopes we could expedite the process. About thirty minutes later a detective named Dickens came to get us. We went into a room with gray stone walls that had a table in the corner of the room along with four chairs, just like I had seen in the movies.

"Again, I'm Detective Dickens, and I will be assessing the accusations you have filed today. So you must be Demarra Hale–the victim. Is that correct?"

"Yes, sir."

"And, ma'am, are you the girl's mother?"

"Yes, I'm Ms. Vause."

"Okay, then let's get started."

"So, Demarra. You are accusing Max and several others of rape, correct? Can you tell me what happened on the night of the incident?"

All the details were in the lengthy report I had just filled out, but he insisted I needed to recount to him what happened, and that he may have some clarifying questions based on what I shared. My first response was to reject this, but I wanted justice so I would do what I had to.

"I want you to be aware of what will happen from this point on.

Max will be contacted about the accusations you have presented today. If he denies what happened he will be asked to take a lie detector test. Once the results of his test come in, you will be notified and asked to come in for an interview. From there, the prosecutor will decide whether to move forward with charges. Do you have any questions for me?"

"How long does the process take?"

"Give or take thirty days."

I had no more questions, but thirty days seemed like an eternity. What gave me peace though was thinking of Max, Dave, and all those other mutherfuckers rotting in jail.

Chapter 6
No Justice, No Peace

By the time I got the call to go to the police station, things had taken a turn for the worse with my mom. I was staying with a nearby neighbor, Blake, and her three sons, who were all at least three years younger than I was. Her oldest, Axel, being the troublemaker he was, would often be the target of Blake's voice that was so loud it seemed to carry over the entire complex. Blake walked with immense force, so that her blonde, stringy hair was always swaying when she moved. If you were close you would hear a thump every time her feet touched the pavement. She never wore shoes, so the soles of her feet were always black. And I don't think I ever saw her without a Mountain Dew, not to mention a cigarette dangling from her mouth. I could never understand the skill it took to keep a cigarette planted in your mouth and yell at the same time, but Blake seemed to pull it off with ease.

I wouldn't say that Blake and my mom were friends, that is, in the sense that one might traditionally think of friendship, but they had each other's backs. They created a bond centered around each other's children which allowed my mom to count on Blake during times when she needed her the most. Like when they drove down Hays Park in the wee hours of the morning looking for me when I didn't come home.

Depression had set in so deeply that I had no desire to go to school, and in fact hadn't been back since I was released from the psychiatric hospital. It wasn't just the depression per se, it was the inability to go back to a place that had once embraced me, but now shunned me. I started to distance myself from many of my friends whom I had known most of my life. The more James and I started to hang out, the more I got to know his friends, who also started to become my friends in a way. My doctor prescribed Zoloft to suppress the numbness I felt, but it didn't seem to help, plus it made me lethargic which I loathed. I had only been on it for a few weeks though, and my doctor said it would take time for me to feel the benefits so I continued to take it in spite of my resistance.

Here I was, at the age of thirteen, sleeping on Blake's cocoa brown couch in her living room, which smelled like pure cigarettes. It was too difficult to be in the presence of my mother, and, well, I had nowhere else to go. At least here I could still see my family, and easily go home if I needed anything since Blake's unit was so close to ours she was like our next door neighbor.

I was enthusiastic about moving forward with pressing charges against Max, Dave, and the others. I couldn't recall the last time I had felt this good. Quite possibly it had been years. I didn't tell my mom about the appointment with the detectives because we weren't really talking and I figured I could manage it on my own. I got on the city bus which I could see from where I lived. When I arrived at the station, I was told to have a seat and the detectives would be with me shortly.

Detective Klein greeted me along with a female detective named Smith. They took me back to the same room that my mom and I had been in a month prior. I sat down at the desk and they began by telling me how much they appreciated me coming in and that Max had taken a lie detector test that revealed he hadn't raped me.

"That's not possible. It happened. I don't care what the results say."

"Demarra, Max told us everything. It's okay. These things happen. You know . . . a girl can like a guy and they not like them and they cry rape."

"I can't speak on behalf of other girls. I'm speaking on behalf of myself. Max raped me. Dave raped me. They all raped me. One by one. Why would I make something like that up?"

"Like I said, it happens sometimes. Max said you've been stalking him for a while. That you're kind of obsessed with him. I get it, he's a nice looking guy."

"Max did rape me. I don't know how these lie detectors work, how accurate they are, all I know is he raped me. It happened at his house. His dad let me in. Did you ask his dad any questions? And Max's brother and his friend witnessed the whole thing. Did you ask them any questions?"

"Demarra, please stop with the lies so we can get on with this."

"Get on with what?"

"Closing your case."

"Closing my case? Just like that? Do you think I would have gone through all this simply to lie? Do you know what it took me to get here? Not just here with the two of you, but here? The pain I have felt? The attempt to take my life? The month I spent in the psychiatric hospital? Even coming down here on my own today. I don't understand why you're treating me like this."

"We're not treating you like anything, just trying to get to the truth, which you seem to refuse to provide us with."

I started to get increasingly agitated. Detective Klein was doing all the talking. I looked at the female detective, Smith, who hadn't uttered a word since I had been there except for her introduction.

"Demarra, I agree with Detective Klein. The results are in. So, let's just move forward so you can go home."

"Moving forward is what I'm trying to do. How do you expect me to do that when you're telling me that Max, and the five boys who raped me, are innocent when I know for a fact they aren't."

"I know how hard it is when you like someone, and they don't like you back. I've been there. It really is okay. Just tell us what really happened."

"I already did. In the long report I provided. That is what happened. Every detail."

"Come on, Demarra. That's not what happened. So just tell us what did."

"I'm not going to tell you it didn't happen because it did. Did you call Tessa, her mom? They can attest to me coming to her house that night. It was like 4 a.m. Did you even contact them?"

"No we didn't because our process is to start with a lie detector test and once a claimed perpetrator passes, bringing the alleged victim in is what we do. That's why you're here."

"So you're telling me that this so-called test is evidence enough for you along with his story even though I have people who can attest to my whereabouts that night, and my whereabouts after."

"That's exactly what we're telling you because, well, we don't believe you."

The room started to close in on me. And the hope I once felt had completely dissipated. I knew that nothing I said was going to make a difference. They had already made up their mind that Max was the victim, not me.

"I don't give a fuck what you believe. I know what happened to me that night, and how dare you suggest otherwise! Max can take all the tests in the world, but he knows what he did, and the five other pieces of shit know what they did to me."

"Settle down. You know we could charge you with falsifying information to a police officer right? So just be honest. We understand and wouldn't do that, but we just wanted you to know what the consequences are for something like this."

"Fuck you and fuck you. It's clear you're not going to help me. You have painted this picture about me that isn't accurate. Shame on you. Shame on you both."

In a state of rage, I threw the folder that held the paperwork I had filed with the help of my mother to attempt to get justice. Considering nothing had been investigated about the legitimacy of my claims, except for the lie detector test and Max's word against mine, there weren't many papers to toss. Then I threw my chair, and the three other empty chairs across the room before storming out. As I walked to the bus stop, covered in tears, I felt hopeless. There was nothing more that could be done. The detectives had determined that I, not Max, was the one at fault and there was absolutely nothing I could do about it. If only I had gone to the police the following morning, if only I hadn't taken a shower, if only I hadn't waited until I was released from the psychiatric hospital to file the report. All I had was if onlys. And if onlys were certainly not going to comfort me. Once I got to the bus stop, I wiped my tears, put some lip gloss on, straightened out my clothes, elongated my posture, and forced a smile. When the bus driver arrived, I greeted him with an exuberant hello, as if I was actually happy, but what I felt was nowhere close to happiness.

The days that followed felt like a black hole that I couldn't seem to get myself out of, and honestly didn't have the strength to even try. The depression medication still didn't help me feel better, and the lethargy increased so I stopped taking it altogether. As a means to continue my treatment, my mother found a Black therapist named Ms. Foster, who was one of the few Black social workers in the area. During our first family session, after I had attended two individual sessions with her, she told my mom that if she didn't get rid of the "bad seed" as she referred to me as, I would destroy my brothers and sister.

"What kind of therapist tells a parent their child is a goner? That change isn't possible? I thought your job was to help us."

"I don't think you can be helped. Look at how you're acting. You don't want help."

"How do you know what I want? You just met me. The third time we are with you, you think you know me? You think you can honestly say that there is no hope for me?"

"I do. In my professional life I've seen a lot. I've worked with all kinds of children just like you and know what I see. You've checked out. And it's not fair for your mother and your siblings to suffer because of you."

"Suffer because of me? I'm hurting. You don't know shit about me, and fuck you for thinking you do."

I got up to leave as she continued to speak. The ringing in my ears prevented me from hearing a word she said. Before I slammed the door, I told that bitch she was the worst therapist ever known to man, and put another "fuck you" on the end.

With no forward path in sight, and a legal requirement for me to be in school, my mother forced me to go back to Hillside Middle School. Begrudgingly I gave in. For the next few weeks I spent most of my time with the school counselor, Ms. Byne, who provided me great comfort, and buffered me from some of the lingering effects of the false rumors about me being a "ho."

And then one day in science, Ms. Timmons, who was one of the few Black teachers in the school, and for some reason made it a point to make my life difficult, pushed me too far. As a result of me not answering correctly in class, she taunted me, and insisted I was stupid for not knowing the answer. And then followed with, "See, this is what you get when you act tough, an unintelligent human," and urged the class not to become that.

"So you're just going to get up in front of the class and call me stupid? You're fucking stupid. Fuck you."

"Get out."

"Oh, you want me to get out of your class? Fuck you. Make me get out."

"Demarra, I'm serious. Leave."

"Like I said, make me leave."

I got up and threw my chair across the room.

"This class is bullshit, and you're a bullshit teacher. People like you should never be allowed to teach."

"Get out and don't come back."

"Oh, don't worry, bitch. I won't be back to your dusty ass class."

I got up, slammed the door behind me, and walked as fast as I could to the counselor's office to see Ms. Byne. I was told she wasn't there and that I could wait until she got back. But I needed to see her now. I needed whatever I was feeling to go away now. I stormed out without responding and ran all the way to the closest girl's bathroom. I broke down on the floor before I couldn't make it to a stall. With my back against the wall, I clenched my legs as tight as I could while my head hung low between my legs and I let the tears flow. The more I told myself to stop crying, or that it was going to be okay, the more I cried. And the more I cried the louder and deeper my cries became.

A few students came into the bathroom and asked if I was okay, but I just kept crying. Clearly I wasn't. Minutes later Ms. Byne appeared and she sat right next to me and wrapped her arms around me. At one point I let out a wail that was unrecognizable to myself. My body began to shake uncontrollably and Ms. Byne held me tighter, repeating over and over again that it was going to be okay, all while calling out to God to *"Please, help this child."* Eventually I let go of my legs and embraced Ms. Byne as I continued to cry until I had nothing left. I had never felt comfort like this.

Chapter 7
Dead Girl Walking

I was immediately pulled out of Hillside and enrolled at Portage North with the goal of being as far away as possible from people who would remind me of what happened that night. Within weeks I realized that Max knew many of the students at Portage North, too. There was no escaping.

Once I realized that Portage North wouldn't be my safe haven after all, my behavior increasingly worsened. In an attempt to feel something, anything, I started to harm myself which began with me piercing my nose myself with a piercing gun, along with nine piercings in my left ear, and four in my right. Those piercings didn't last long since many of them got infected and I had to allow them to close, but I was able to preserve my nose piercing.

Once the principal caught wind that I had pierced my nose, I was called into his office and urged to remove it. Although I knew little about African history, I shared that piercings were indigenous to Africa and if they were going to force me to remove it then they were being discriminatory. Considering the school barely had any students of color, let alone Black students, I was allowed to keep it.

I also started burning myself with the metal part of my lighter. I'd ignite the lighter and keep it lit for about a minute and then place it on my skin until the flesh melted. Although this was painful, I felt comfort in the pain. Those few seconds allowed me to know that I was alive.

I worked hard to get back in the groove of school, but I never really found my rhythm again. Up until recently, I had enjoyed learning, my teachers, and being in school, but I was disinterested in anything other than activities that would allow me to escape my life. That caused me to begin running away from home more frequently which landed me in the juvenile home after I had been missing or "on the run" for weeks. The first time I was detained in a juvenile facility, I discovered I had chlamydia.

When I first ran away, I stayed with James on Hays Park. We had been dating since I left the psychiatric unit. By the end of the first week we had sex for the first time, which was my first consensual sexual encounter. Although I didn't enjoy it, and honestly felt nothing but discomfort from it, I liked James so I was happy that he seemed to be pleased by it.

After a couple weeks of being at James' and not only witnessing his rage but having his rage directed at me, I left. I jumped from house to house on Hays Park, giving the only thing I thought I had to give in order to be sheltered and fed. Word got around quickly. By the end I ended up having sex with five people.

The roughly thirty days I resided at the juvenile home were seemingly pleasant. Although I had to sleep in a locked cell with a small window that was too high for me to see out of, and sleep on an uncomfortable mattress that was on the floor with a heavy blue blanket that made me itch, the quiet gave me peace. I especially appreciated the nights when someone would come in from the

Kalamazoo Public Library to read to us. This took me to a place far away from where I dwelled. And although those thirty minutes would go by quickly, I felt both respite and new possibility in those moments.

Reading was something I always enjoyed. I read so many books in fact, that I always far exceeded the reading requirement for the *Book It* program, which meant I never missed out on a Pizza Hut personal pan pizza, and whatever other perks came along with the program. *Charlotte's Web* by E.B. White grew to be my all time favorite.

When I was released from the juvenile home, I had to go and live with my uncle Haba, his wife, Chikere, and their two children. I was now in ninth grade, and based on where they lived, I would be enrolling at Kalamazoo Central. I feared I would run into many of the people I went to Hillside with. My fear materialized nearly the instant I walked into the school. By the time I made it to class I had run into more than ten people I knew. As time went on I became more and more withdrawn and skipped school every chance I got. I was smoking roughly a pack of cigarettes a day and marijuana periodically.

Living with Chikere and Haba made my depression spiral, but if I showed any signs of distress, I was told I should be grateful they were taking care of me, and how miserable my life would be if it wasn't for them. These weren't the words of Haba, but he never really seemed to interject when Chikere would go on and on about this, so they seemed to be his words, too.

Chikere was an avid runner and was tenacious about her diet which resulted in a figure that didn't look like she had brought any children into the world. She often made comments about my appearance in comparison to hers, and that I shouldn't have any excuses–alluding to the fact that I needed to lose weight. She monitored what I ate, and ensured that my portion sizes were minimal. She also insisted that I start working out on their treadmill. When it seemed that no matter what I ate or how I moved didn't get the results that Chikere expected, the comments about my size increased. In a state of desperation, I began throwing up after meals so I could become what Chikere wanted me to be.

The first time I stuck my fingers down my throat to rid myself of the meticulously portioned dinner I had just consumed, I told myself that it would just be this one time. I told myself the same lie the next time. It was painful to jab my index and middle finger into my throat, and my body would convulse as I forced the food to come up. The acidic aftertaste was horrible, but this practice became part of my daily routine. After every meal and snack, I would enter the bathroom and turn on the water so no one could hear what I was doing. Or I would make sure no one was around, like when I was at school. Chikere's positive attention to my transformed figure made me feel like she was finally seeing me.

Chikere would often berate Haba when he wasn't around, making it known how much better his life was with her in it. She would go on and on about the women he had dated before her, especially, Paka, his first wife, whom he had Akpan with. I had grown up around Paka and Akpan so we were quite close. Chikere, and her children, on the other hand, I barely knew because she rarely brought them around us.

She would talk to me about what her life was like before she met Haba, as if we were friends, and that she could have had anyone, but she chose him and as a result it was his duty to fall in line with whatever she wanted. And whatever she wanted, she got. She often bragged about this. One day she even showed me more than twenty credit cards she had which bought the exclusive name-brand clothes she insisted she and her children have. She stayed home and Haba worked tirelessly to provide for them, and now me. Their possessions were nicer than anything we had owned. And although they lived in a trailer park, it was a luxury one so it didn't really seem like a trailer park at all.

By this time, Dayo had moved to Denver, Colorado with the *Americorps* program. Although we fought tenaciously over the years, I missed her fiercely. I missed all my family. I never quite fit in with Haba and his family. Even when we sat in the living room to watch television, I was slightly away from everyone–either on a stool or at a small bistro table adjacent to the kitchen. On my birthday Dayo sent me a card with a hand-written note expressing how much she loved me. For some reason I felt especially low this day, and her words were just what I needed. I sat in silence after I read the card and headed to bed early. That night I read the card over and over again until I cried myself to sleep. I desperately wanted to escape this new hell that had become my life.

It all came to an end after Chikere's niece, who was babysitting, caught me smoking a cigarette in my bedroom. I pleaded for her not to tell, but she did anyway. Chikere whopped me with immense force that evening, bare ass and all. I cried not just because of the physical pain but I was also humiliated. Haba was nowhere in sight.

After that my mother allowed me to come back home. I started skipping school and running away even more frequently which landed me back in the juvenile home for a couple weeks. And then on my fourteenth birthday, I got caught stealing at Hudson's department store which resulted in house arrest and involved a black tether I had to wear around my ankle for weeks. I also had to undergo frequent check-ins with my probation officer, Fenem Billups. Not to mention, I had to pay fines and complete community service before Fenem deemed me ready to fully re-enter society as a free citizen.

The last time I was in juvenile detention wasn't even for something I did. My friend Alice and I had gone out to the terrace to smoke marijuana. When we arrived back in the house Alice noticed her mom's purse was in the living room. She made sure the coast was clear and then went into her purse to get her ATM card.

"Girl, what the fuck are you doing?"

"We are about to go kick it. I know the code. We'll get some money out of the ATM."

"What if your mom needs to use her bank card?"

"I'll tell her we're walking to the store and will be right back. She isn't going anywhere, girl. She has to work tonight. She's probably in her room sleeping right now. "

"Okay, if you say so."

Alice checked in her mom's room to confirm she was sleeping. Once she verified she was, we headed on foot to the ATM. Alice withdrew $140. We walked back to her house hours before her mother was up from her nap. Once her mom left, Alice called one of her older guy friends to pick us. Alice was on top of the world since she was buying for all of us. The money she had stolen was gone by the time we crept back to her house at 3 a.m.

Weeks later I discovered that Alice's mom realized the money was missing from her account. Instead of Alice fessing up to what she had done, she blamed me for the whole thing. Although the camera showed I was simply with Alice, somehow I took the rap for her actions by association, while Alice went scot-free. This landed me with my third set of charges and back into the juvenile home as part of my sentencing.

There would be many occasions where my white friends would attempt to pin things on me, or I was deemed to be a bad influence, although they were often the culprits, and I was merely along for the ride.

Alice and I never spoke again after that. There had been too many occasions where it was clear that Alice was about Alice. The previous time should have been the last time.

Three weeks earlier I headed to Alice's to hang out after school. After going to Taco Bell to get some food, Alice convinced her mom to drop us off at the apartment where Marcus lived. Alice had a way of convincing her mother to do whatever she wanted to do. That meant we could drink alcohol and smoke cigarettes and weed as long as we did it in her presence. And even when she'd tell Alice "no," her mom would quickly concede because she would become verbally and physically violent. We told her we were going to see one of our girlfriends and we would call her when we were ready to be picked up. Once we arrived, we were offered some beer and asked if we wanted to play cards. I had only played a few card games before and I wasn't particularly good at them, but I agreed anyway. Alice was on Sean's team, the guy she liked, and I was on Marcus's team. After getting a tutorial from Marcus on how to play spades, we played a few rounds, and then Sean suggested we play for incentives.

"What type of incentives?"

"What kind of incentives do you want to play for?"

"I don't know. You're the one who suggested it."

"How about for sex."

"What do you mean by sex?"

"The losing team has to have sex with their partner."

"That's ridiculous. Right, Alice?"

"Yeah, I guess a little, but this will be fun."

"No it won't be fun. So you're telling me that if you lose you'll be okay with having sex with Sean?"

"Sure, why not?"

"Because we're talking about exchanging sex for a card game."

"Yeah, Demarra, but it's just sex."

Sex wasn't just sex to me. Or maybe it was. It never had significant meaning to me, actually. I didn't even enjoy having sex. I just did it because that's what I discovered you did in relationships. If you were dating, sex would inevitably be on the menu. Whether I liked it or not, I saw it as my duty.

Marcus started egging me on saying that he was really good at playing cards so there was no way we would lose. It wasn't what my partner said that made me reconsider, it was the fact that I figured no one would actually go through with such a ludicrous idea so I reluctantly agreed. After Marcus and I lost a few rounds, I started to become a little uneasy. Marcus picked up on this and started to console me.

"Don't worry, girl. Anything can happen from here."

Sean chimed in, "Look at you, looking all scared and stuff."

"I'm not scared," I lied.

"That's not what I'm sensing. I can smell the fear from here."

"Leave her alone, Sean," Alice chimed in with a laugh.

"Yeah, man, chill out. Be cool," said Marcus.

"He is just talking shit right now. Everyone talks shit while playing cards. You'll see that the more you play."

"It's fine."

"Oh. It's fine. You're telling me you're not a little scared that you will lose. Remember you will have to sleep with my boy if you do. My guess is you don't really want to do that over a little card game, do you?"

"I know what I signed up for."

"So you're trying to be tough? We'll see how tough you are when we win this game."

"Whatever."

"Why are you being such a jerk?" asked Alice.

"You're tripping. I'm not. Your girl is just trying to act all hard. I'm not feeling that."

"You don't need to be feeling anything. Why are you so focused on her anyway?"

"I'm not. Just saying."

"Alright, we all heard you. Can we get back to the card game now? It's your deal," said Marcus.

Sean didn't reply, but shuffled and dealt the cards as requested. This round went a little better than the last round, but not enough to give me much hope that we would win the game.

It was now Marcus's turn to deal the cards. I looked down at my hand. I didn't have much to play with. Together we said the maximum we could get would be six. Even if we got the six books we still couldn't win the game. It was hopeless. I played the game out to the end forcing myself to smile the entire time. Once the last play was made, it was official, we had lost.

"Y'all got served," said Sean. "Good game, Alice."

"Sorry, Demarra, We tried. You played a good game too, especially for your first time."

"Thanks," I said dryly.

"So you know what comes next, right?" said Sean.

I laughed hoping that everyone would join in on the laughter, instead there was dead silence.

"Girl, we're serious. We don't play when it comes to bets," said Sean.

"Can we negotiate something else? I'll look in my purse to see how much cash I have."

"No, we're not accepting any cash, right Marcus?!?! You expect to get your payment in full now, right man?"

"Right," said Marcus hesitantly.

"Marcus, I don't think you mean that. I'm not that kind of girl. I can't just sleep with you on arranged terms. I'm not wired like that. Plus with everyone around. It just wouldn't be right."

"Then why would you agree to the terms of our bet?" said Marcus. "If you had no intention of sleeping with me, why would you agree to do it? That's not cool. Makes me think you play games."

"I know how it must seem, but I thought it was a bluff. I didn't think you guys were serious, serious. I thought we'd get to the end of the game and have some good laughs and then keep it moving."

"Naw, sorry. We fully expect you to keep your end of the deal. Alice and I won the card game. If we hadn't she and I would be in the same position you and Marcus are in now."

"Can't you guys give her another chance?" chimed Alice. "It was a stupid, naïve mistake."

"Sorry, but no. Now go on in there and do your business. We'll be out here waiting until you're done."

I looked at Marcus. I could tell he didn't want to go through with it either, yet he was under an enormous amount of pressure from Sean. I figured he didn't want to seem weak. To give in to me would somehow go against his manhood. Still the thought of us having sex in his room while everyone else stayed in the other room listening was unbearable. I burst into tears.

"Marcus, please. I can't do this. It was dumb of me to agree to it. I will do something else, just name it. Anything other than something sexual I will do for you, but please don't make me sleep with you."

"Let's just get it over with. You did agree to doing it. I don't want to make this any harder for you than what it has to be. Stop crying. Everything is going to be okay."

"No it won't be okay. You don't understand. I can't do it. I won't do it."

"Yes, you will. You said you would, and now you want to play all innocent and shit? If you were so innocent you wouldn't have agreed to do it," said Sean.

"I know what it looks like. I'm not that girl though. This is just a case of poor judgment."

"Poor judgment or not, you agreed to do it."

"Marcus can decide. I am begging you. Please don't make me do this."

The look in his eyes indicated he actually felt bad for me, but his words contradicted that.

"Sean is right. You should have never agreed to it if you weren't planning on doing it. Enough talking, let's go back to my room and get this over with."

He grabbed my arm gently to get me up from the table. I continued to cry as we walked back to his room. The thought crossed my mind to leave but instead fear set in, just like it did the night of my gang rape. Although this was under different circumstances, it felt like déjà vu. We entered the room which was quite dark since night had fallen. I was glad he didn't turn the lights on. I loathed the idea of him seeing my naked body.

"Girl, stop crying. It will be over soon."

"Marcus, please, please don't make me do this. You don't understand. Please."

"I do understand. I know you don't want to do this. I'll be gentle. Come here."

My feet were planted firmly in the carpet. I couldn't move. He came in my direction, and delicately placed his hands on the outside of the top of my arms and moved his face towards mine. Every part of my body tensed up.

"Don't say anything. I'm not going to make you go through with this. Just go with it. They need to believe that we actually did it," he whispered in my ear. Then said out loud, "Now girl, hush with all that crying and take your clothes off. I'll be gentle I promise."

"As long as you're gentle," I replied.

"Now come on over here and get in the bed. Do you like it on top or the bottom?"

"The bottom is fine."

"Protection is a must. Hold on a second."

Marcus opened a condom wrapper, took the condom out and then placed both in the garbage can next to his bed. He then started to make kissing noises, and I started to do the same. By this point, the crying had ceased. This lasted for a couple minutes. He moved to my ear again.

"Now you need to continue to go with me on this. I know it will be awkward, but I am doing this for you so you have to do this for me. I can't let on to my friends that I'm soft in any shape or form. I am going to start moaning and moving the bed. I need you to start doing the same. Just follow my lead. Cool?"

"Yes," I whispered.

"Oh, girl, you like that?"

"Yes. Keep going."

"Uh huh. I think I hit your spot."

"Yes, yes."

We continued this for another ten minutes to make it believable. I vowed to never say anything, not even to Alice. I desperately wanted to tell her the kindness Marcus had bestowed upon me, but I knew I couldn't for his sake. Alice talked too much in general, but if I made her angry, then she would definitely go blabbing to Sean.

I walked out of the room, refusing to make eye contact with anyone else except for Alice, and grabbed my stuff. Before I walked out the door, I asked Alice if she was ready. She said she'd call her mom right away and she'd be here in no time. I told her I'd wait outside.

As I walked down the stairs to the floor level, the thought that everyone believed we had sex made me sick to my stomach. I nearly lost my breath which caused me to sit down once I got to the last stair before I hurled all the Taco Bell I had eaten earlier.

I was grateful that Marcus showed me compassion. I was determined to never step foot in that apartment again. There was no way I could face Sean or Marcus, no matter how kind he ultimately had been to me.

No one followed me outside to check on me—not even Alice. By the time she came out of the house, I was already in the car waiting for her. There was silence as we drove home. Once we were in the safety of Alice's room we didn't speak of the incident. She never brought up Sean around me again. As I lay in Alice's bed, all I kept thinking was how close a call that had been.

Chapter 8
The Voices In My Head

I had dodged a bullet that night with Alice, but unfortunately there would be many times that I wouldn't be so lucky, especially as my drug and alcohol consumption increased. When I enrolled at one of the alternative high schools my access to drugs and alcohol became infinite. I could get anything I wanted, pretty much anytime I wanted, as long as I had the money to pay for it. Many times I simply received free access simply by association.

At school, we had smoke breaks in the courtyard. Although you were supposed to be eighteen to smoke, no one monitored us so we all smoked. Plus I could leave campus to indulge in marijuana between classes and not worry about getting kicked out of school when I came back smelling like cannabis.

I had also managed to get a fake ID which allowed me to get into nightclubs. I would get so inebriated I would often pass out wherever I was sitting and my friends would have to walk me out of wherever we were hanging out. And when house parties were involved, I would get so drunk and high that I often woke up the next day on someone's couch or bed.

The more I immersed myself in party life, the more things became strained with my mother. Between the fights with my siblings and my refusal to follow the rules, being kicked out of the house became routine. The non-stop violent fights I'd have with Dayo and Jonbenet would result in the police being called to our home often. When Dayo returned from Colorado the fights got worse. The main reason for fights with Dayo was that I would often wear her clothes without permission and ruin them by either stretching them out, because I was bigger than she was, or getting them stained.

The weekend before my prom, my sister hit a tipping point after she discovered I destroyed a Guess outfit she had just purchased. For her it wasn't just that I had taken her things with no regard for her, but it was the hard work she put into purchasing what she wanted. Ever since we were about 10 years old, we were pretty much on our own to purchase new clothes because of our mom's limited income. It wasn't that my mother didn't buy us anything but it was restricted to a few outfits at places she could afford to shop, like Kmart or Goodwill. The name brands we desired, and our friends coveted, were never accessible to us through her. This meant that, at the age of thirteen, my sister started working in the cornfield to earn money, and at the age of fourteen I was cleaning rooms at a nearby hotel.

When I came home from school and entered my room I was flabbergasted to see that everything I owned, except for my plum prom dress, sparkly jewelry, and black shoes were gone. Enraged, I sprinted down the steps to confront my mother about my belongings. She told me matter of factly that she and Dayo had bagged up my things and taken them to a shelter. She then said that hopefully now I would learn that it wasn't okay to take other people's things. I wasn't hearing any of it, and insisted they go back and get my stuff. My mother was adamant that it wasn't going to happen and I went so ballistic that she grabbed a knife, possibly for fear that I would attack her, and told me to leave. At that time I had nowhere to go, and no money to support me or replace all the things I had lost. I had worked for years to accumulate everything I had once owned. I begged and pleaded to stay home. I vowed to do better. But it was too late. My mother called my school counselor, Katie Howard, and she was at our door about thirty minutes later. She graciously allowed me to live with her, her husband Marc, who was also an educator, and her daughter, Madeline, for the summer. One of the first things we did was go to Target to get a few items I could wear until I earned enough money from my job at Subway to begin replenishing what I had lost.

That summer at Katie's was such a gift. They had a huge house in a historic neighborhood. Although I had seen many homes like Katie's I had never actually been in one. Everything was beautifully decorated. There was artwork plastered on the walls, which coordinated with the rainbow pops of color that filled each room, and fresh flowers. Katie worked hard to integrate me into their home life to the extent she could. Although Marc was kind to me, he was less inclusive than Katie was–although he never did anything overtly that made me feel less than for being a guest in their home, with very little to contribute.

I quickly realized there was tension in their relationship from the way they interacted with each other. The bickering was fairly constant and they rarely spent time with each other. This was further exacerbated when Katie revealed to me she liked Thenga, who worked at the school. I had known Thenga since I was a little girl. In fact, the mother of his children and their two girls lived in the building adjacent to ours in Evergreen South.They moved in just a couple years after we did. Thenga would get the kids in the neighborhood together to play group games in the field that was behind their building. The field was so large it bordered his and four other buildings and the second playground in the complex in somewhat of a triangle formation. He not only gathered us, but he also partook in the fun. Thenga was the only adult in the complex who did, so I liked him instantly. But he, like most fathers in the complex, came and went, or were altogether absent from the lives of their children.

Although I knew staying with Katie was temporary, there was a part of me that wanted to stay. I didn't want to be part of Katie's family per se, but this was the first time I felt settled in years. After about six weeks of living with Katie and her family, I discovered I had crabs. I had been seeing a guy named Jackson who I contracted it from. Katie was furious for having to ferociously clean everything, not just in my room, but anything I had come in contact with in their home. No matter how many times I said I was sorry, and worked to make it right, my presence in their home had become too much for them to bear. My summer with them was cut short and I ended up back with my mom, right before my junior year.

Issues ensued with my mom and I found myself in and out of

friends' homes much of the time since home didn't feel like a place I was welcome. I would sometimes stay at friends' houses for upwards of three weeks at a time. I went to Katie to see what it would take for me to graduate from high school early. She confirmed that if I was diligent in not failing any of my classes and worked in the office to earn extra credits I could be done by the end of junior year. And that's exactly what I was determined to do.

Community high school in some ways provided a safe haven that felt far away from the life I had always known, but slowly it became clear that many of my friends were also connected to Max, Dave and friends of their friends. Once again, I couldn't break free from the past, no matter how hard I tried. Even some of my closest friends had hung out with Max in the past and thought he was a decent guy. This put me in the position of explaining or defending myself in the moments when my gang rape came up. There was even a time when we went to a house where Max was and he taunted me while I stood in silence with my head hung low. Our "mutual friends" never interjected, nor stood up for me. This somehow never stopped me from spending time with them, although I never had contact with Max again after that.

By the end of my junior year, I had experimented with nearly every illicit drug that had been introduced to the world. This included hallucinogens, meth, and cocaine. I even smoked crack the night of my high school graduation. I didn't like the way crack made me feel, and my drug of choice quickly became cocaine. While my access to cocaine increased exponentially, many of my friends started using heroin. I had been open to trying nearly anything but there was something about heroin that made me afraid to try it. Heroin use had become so bad in my circle that many of my friends had become addicted to it, including Carter with whom I had gone to my last prom. When he started his detox process he was dating my friend Emelia. Her parents were out of town that weekend and she locked Carter in her bedroom at his request until the drugs were out of his system to the point that he no longer craved them.

Not only had my drug use increased but my alcohol consumption had become out of control. I drank as if it were my life support. As if I drank enough of it, it would quench my thirst. I'd throw back a fifth of liquor like it was sport. I drank quickly and I fell promptly into a state that caused me to do things I never imagined, often regretted, and at times, couldn't bounce back from. The tipping point was on the dawn of my sixteenth birthday when my mother found me passed out in the lawn and soaked in my own urine. Later that day I was forced to check into rehab where I stayed for a few weeks before being kicked out for having an altercation with one of the female residents in my unit.

Once back home, I tried my best to keep the peace, but I knew I was ready to live on my own. About a month before I graduated from high school I convinced my mom to cosign a lease so I could live in Knollwood apartments for the summer. She agreed to it as long as I could find a roommate. Western Michigan University students who lived in Knollwood would go back to wherever they came from for the summer which allowed people like me to swoop in for three months at deeply reduced rent before they returned to start school again. Once my friend Joanna agreed, we proceeded with the arrangements and in early June we moved in. This was the summer before I turned seventeen.

Although I would be responsible for paying my own rent, about a year before I graduated my mom started saving the $50 per month my father paid in child support. This resulted in a gift of $600 the day after I graduated to start life on my own, which I was super grateful for. I figured that as long as I had Joanna, my job at the ice cream shop at the mall, and the money I'd get back from federal student aid from Kalamazoo Valley Community College, we'd have all the resources we needed to not just stay in Knollwood, but also move into our next place.

The first weekend we moved in we had an epic house party. In fact, nearly every night, we'd have people over or we'd venture off to someone else's house to engage in a night of fun. I'd stay up most of the night, sleep a few hours, head to campus for classes, work my shift, and do it all over again.

My cocaine use started to increase quite a bit since nearly every social circle of mine had access to it. The supply was so plentiful that I never even had to buy it. I started to get frequent nosebleeds from my increased use, and had become thinner and thinner as a result of the way cocaine suppressed my appetite. I also started to lash out at the world more. This didn't become fully clear to me until one day I was coming home from meeting the mother of a guy I had been seeing named Gamal. I had a crush on Gamal for years but he hadn't given me much attention until that summer, in part because I was much younger than him, which would've made it illegal for him to date me when we first met. When we made it to the point of meeting his mother, which he never introduced anyone to before, I thought for sure we were starting to build something that could be really special. When we came back to my place, a woman in my complex confronted me about something and Gamal had to hold me back from fighting her. Once inside my apartment, Gamal told me that he couldn't date someone with a temper like mine which was unfortunate because he really liked me. I tried to justify my actions by explaining that she was in the wrong and I was simply defending myself. He said he understood that, and that I was right, but the fact he couldn't calm me down made him feel like I was out of control. And then he left. I was crushed.

That night Joanna and I went to a house party and I snorted about ten lines of cocaine—the most I had ever done in one night. I could barely stand up. I fell down the stairs on a few occasions and had several repeat conversations with individuals at the party since my short-term memory seemed to go completely out the window. Around 7 a.m., Joanna's mom came to pick us up from the party, and took us to McDonalds for breakfast, which I thought would curb this hangover unlike any I had ever experienced. Once home I slept for a few hours before I had to get up so my sister Dayo could take me to the grocery store.

When she arrived she commented on how thin I had gotten since the last time she saw me. Not to mention, how sickly I looked. I brushed it off although I knew she was right. My 150 pound frame had withered down to 115 which for some would have been a dream come true but for me it was a sign that something was gravely wrong. On top of my drug use, I barely slept. I averaged about three hours a night, on top of my rigorous schedule which entailed summer courses at the community college and working as much as I could. I was sick, but I didn't want the outside world to know which included Dayo.

As we walked through the aisles and bantered as only sisters can, I started to feel nauseous. I left my cart with Dayo and sped walked to the bathroom. Once inside, I caught a glimpse of myself in the mirror and stopped dead in my tracks. As I examined myself it was as if I was looking at someone else. I appeared to be lifeless. It was as if the light had been sucked right out of me. My skin hadn't been this pale since I was a little girl, long before I basked in the sun for hours during summers.

Thoughts started flashing through my mind of all that had happened the past several years.

These thoughts caused me to nearly hyperventilate. I was disgusted by the image looking back at me so I looked away. For once, what had always been there, came to the light, so visceral I could nearly touch it. I hated myself, what I had become, what quite possibly I had always been. There was a time when I loved myself, the world, and everything in it. From birth, there was a light I embodied and it was manifested in everything around me. At least that's what my mother used to say. It didn't take long to squander that zest I felt for life. I wanted to know how I got to this point. I mean, of course I knew on some level, but I wanted change and convinced myself if I could get clear then change could potentially be possible.

I begrudgingly looked at myself again in the mirror. My emaciated existence made me convulse. After two jerks, I moved as quickly as I could to the stall to rid myself of the McDonalds I had eaten that morning and anything still in my system from the day before. No matter how hard I tried to purge myself of what was now, or what had been before, I couldn't get my body to react the way it normally would when I put my fingers down my throat. I had done this so many times before–it was commonplace–as routine as waking up, brushing my teeth, eating, sleeping, and yet now, nothing. So I just sat on the toilet and hoped I would eventually throw up so I could get on with my day.

The voices that had periodically played out in the background for as long as I could remember were now screaming at me. Normally I could quiet these voices with busyness or substances or relationships, but this time I had none of those things. I was completely and utterly alone.

These were the same voices that had taunted me since the

beginning, yet I had been in a place where I could rationalize with them. Who I used to believe I really was would always triumph over the voices that told me I was a lesser version of myself. Lately, however, these voices had become more constant. I'd wake up with them, go to sleep with them, they'd follow me into the bathroom, be with me on the bus, taunt me while I was walking across the street, be the silent third party during conversations with others. I considered finally giving in, listening for once to who they told me I was and all the things I would never be.

You're not good enough.

You will never amount to anything.

You might as well just give up now.

You'll never be worthy.

The world and everyone in it would be better without you.

No one loves you . . .

Certainly I wasn't lovable, I mean, who would love me? Especially after all that I had done. I dared to look in the mirror again desperately looking for answers. Maybe if I looked at myself long enough I could love myself. If I could love me then maybe others could love me too. I stared long and hard at myself, the tears flowing from my eyes like that waterfall I saw once in an Encyclopedia. The image was so beautiful. I wish I could be like that waterfall. Free. Freedom. Free spirit. Free will. Fuck free will. I didn't even know if I believed in free will. I desperately wanted to though. The idea that I could choose, at this very moment, a new path. I'd like a new path. I wondered where it would lead me. Then I thought of the yellow brick road from *The Wizard of Oz*. A distant memory popped into my head. So vivid; it was as if I was there experiencing it all over again.

Mrs. Yo, my third grade teacher loved me from the very beginning. Her eyes said so the instant I met her. She understood things about me that I never had to come out and say. She saw me, really saw me, and I was grateful for this. My first encounter with the arts was because of her. The Wizard of Oz at the Civic Auditorium was magical. This experience was different from anything I had ever seen or imagined. The characters made me fall in love with stories. I had always been an avid reader, but this was different. No story I had ever read compared to the real thing. It was like reading a story in 3D. Seeing the costumes, hearing the words roll off the tongues of the actors and actresses. I was captivated. I wanted more. I wished I could pocket this moment–take it with me wherever I went. Yes, it would be my safe haven. I'd find my way, just like Dorothy had found hers. I looked up at Mrs. Yo and I was overtaken by joy. This was love. The audience began to fade, then the actors, the stage, and everything around me until there was no building at all. Then there was just me and Mrs. Yo. We exchanged one last smile, both of our hearts full. And then there was just me, alone, nothing but blackness surrounding me.

The blackness eventually dissipated and I was brought back to reality. Back to the bathroom at Meijer.

"Shut up," I yelled but the voices simply got louder so I got louder,

too. Through this madness, I heard an unfamiliar voice ask, *"Are you okay?"* I had no idea anyone had even come into the bathroom. I didn't respond out of fear, but just sat there and continued to cry. The woman asked me a few more times before she said she was going to get help and then rapidly exited. That forced me to panic. I didn't want anyone to see me in the condition I was in. I just needed a little time to sort out my thoughts. After about a minute, I unlocked the stall and went back to the mirror thinking I would be more satisfied this time with the image looking back, but I wasn't. In fact, I felt an even greater disdain than before. My body weakened and I slowly slithered to the bathroom floor. My thoughts now filled with the night of my gang rape. I tried with all the effort in my body to resist the thoughts. I wanted to move past them, but they were such an intricate part of me. It was the memory that overtook all memories. And with that, I gave in just like I always did. I was that 13-year-old girl all over again and they were the young men who nearly shattered my existence.

Chapter 9
Primal Urges

The woman who had once been there returned, but this time she was with the police and Dayo. The officers were adamant that I needed to be psychologically assessed but Dayo convinced them that I was simply having an extremely rough day. She assured them she would take me right home and all would be well. As we walked through the grocery store all eyes were on us as the officers escorted us out of the building. When we got to the car Dayo and I sat in silence which dragged on until we arrived back at my apartment complex.

"Demarra, what the fuck was that?"

"I don't know."

"What do you mean you don't know? You could have been sent to the psychiatric hospital. Is that what you want?"

"Of course not."

"So why would you do that? Act like that?"

"I'm tired."

"Tired? Are you not getting enough rest?"

"No, I'm not, but that's not the kind of tiredness I'm talking about."

"So what is it?"

"Life."

"Okay. What does that mean?"

"It means that I don't know if I want to be here anymore."

"I'm not sure what you mean."

"You know what that means."

"Demarra, what is the problem? You have a lot of things going for yourself. You have an apartment, are in college. You graduated early so you could have the life you have right now. What more do you want? It just never seems like enough for you."

"Why do you have to do that?"

"Do what?"

"Make me feel like I shouldn't feel the way I do."

"Well, I just don't get it. You have freedom now. Are doing your own thing. You got what you wanted so what's the problem?"

"The problem is I feel empty."

"Empty? I don't get it."

"I know you don't."

"What's that supposed to mean?"

"It means you don't really know me, see me."

"I'm here, aren't I?"

"Yeah, right now you are."

"I've always been here."

"No, Dayo, you haven't."

"When have I not been there for you? I've always supported you."

"I know you think so, but you haven't."

"Here we go. I have been here. Aren't I here now? Haven't I always showed up for you?"

"You left."

"I had to leave. I needed to get out of here. Start my own life."

"I needed you. You have no idea how much I needed you. I've been alone."

"You never really wanted my support, Demarra. Do you recall our childhood? How you pushed me away? How you repeatedly went against me? Constantly fought me? How you took and ruined my clothes? How dare you say I wasn't there for you?!? I even came to your rescue when you got caught stealing. That's bullshit, Demarra."

"You're right, but that didn't mean I didn't want you there. I just wanted mom. I didn't want you to be our mother figure. I wanted you to be my sister. I resented you for filling in the gaps when mom couldn't because she was working or out shopping or whatever she was doing when she was gone for hours."

"I wanted mom, too. How do you think I felt? I didn't want the responsibility of taking care of you and Jonbenet. That was a lot on me. Especially because neither one of you listened to me and often fought against me. How do you think that was for me?"

"I never thought of that."

"I know because all you ever do is think of yourself. It's always about you. Who hurt you. Who's done you wrong. Well, I was hurt, too. That's why I had to leave. I had to choose myself for once."

I didn't know how to respond. I knew she was right. Of course she had endured pain, just as I had, just as we all had.

"I didn't realize me leaving impacted you so much. I'm sorry. I wasn't leaving you. I thought of you all often."

"I believe that. I got your birthday card and your note really touched me. I was at one of my lowest points when I was living with Haba & Chikere. And receiving your card that day lifted my spirit."

"I wanted nothing more than to protect you, but realized very early that I wouldn't be able to. And honestly, it wasn't ultimately my job, although, as your big sister, I desperately wanted to."

"Thank you for saying that. I believe you. And I'm sorry it's taken me so long to see that you were also a victim of our childhood. None of us were safe."

"No, we weren't, but yet we're here, and we can find safety within ourselves."

"I'd love to believe that, sis, and yet I don't feel safe."

"I get that, but today is just today. Tomorrow can be the start of something different. Even this moment can be pivotal towards the creation of a new life for you."

"Yeah."

"I know you don't believe me because all you can see is the pain of the moment, but when you decide to make different choices you will see that your life can be great. You can be happy, And you can feel a sense of security. And I'll be here in the meantime. I'll always be here."

We hugged each other tightly before I got out of the car and exchanged an *"I love you."* As I walked to my door, although the loneliness was still palpable, I felt a glimpse of hope.

At the end of the summer, I moved in with my friend Hailey, and continued to work at the ice cream shop. Life felt like it was finally moving in the right direction until the day we drove to Lansing to visit her boyfriend, Jaari, at Michigan State University. This was her first visit since he left for college earlier that summer. They had only been dating a few months, but Hailey was sure Jaari was the one.

On the way to see him, a black BMW rode beside us in the opposite lane and the front passenger kept trying to get our attention. He rolled his window down and kept pleading with us to pull over because he just had to meet me. Initially we thought they were just joking around, but eventually it became clear that they were genuinely interested. Hailey pulled to the side of the highway and they followed.

I discovered that the guy who was adamant to meet me was Trenton. He was obviously much older than I was, very handsome with toffee colored skin, wavy black hair that he wore in a fade, and he was tall–at least six feet. He wore black from head to toe except for a white button up dress shirt, with a dark gray wool trench. Gold adorned nearly every finger along with a gold necklace that had a big cross that hit the middle of his chest and a diamond stud in each ear. I had perused countless fashion magazines and what he wore was clearly similar to the designer stuff I had seen.

He told me he had never asked someone to pull over so he could meet them before, but he was so captivated by my beauty he just had to try to meet me. I hung onto every word. I had countless boys and men that had been attracted to me over the years, but my relationship with them was lukewarm at best. Even when I had boyfriends whom I thought I liked, my connection to them was quite lackluster. I had sex simply because it was a perfunctory act, and the only way I knew how to connect with them, but I never got any real pleasure out of it. Sex was so meaningless to me, in fact, that I had accumulated nearly seventy sexual partners, yet had never had an orgasm. And since I had no sense of my body, I also had no way of helping my partners get me there.

As this man spoke to me, something in me ignited. I felt that possibly for the first time I had met a man who could actually love me, really love me. Every male I had come in contact with had hurt me. Every relationship ended badly because I would leave when it was clear I was being manipulated or when physical abuse was on the horizon. Like when I tried to leave Jamie's after we had a big fight and he used physical force to try to get me to stay. Needless to say, I never saw him again after that.

One thing I knew for sure is that I would not be in a physically abusive relationship. Emotional and verbal abuse was something I had tolerated much longer than I should have, however. With Mitch for example, it took a year before I finally left the relationship. By the time I left, he refused to give me any of the things I had at his house, including my CK One cologne which I loved. He also called me every name in the book in the process, simply because I decided I no longer wanted to be with him due to the poor way he was treating me.

I had done my fair share of harm in relationships, too. I flirted, and sometimes slept with other people behind the backs of guys I was dating-some of whom were their friends. I certainly wasn't proud of this, but I had no sense of what it meant to be loyal. When it was all said and done, I hated myself for this. I had lost relationships with people who really cared about me as a result, but my urges seemed to overtake any feelings I had for them. These actions were primal. And it was as if males could see this in me. Sometimes when they paid attention to me, I latched on. I would try to resist since I truly didn't want to hurt anyone, but occasionally, no matter how hard I tried, I fell prey to temptation.

The more Trenton spoke, the more I was convinced that I needed to get to know this man. I had met another man named Chester at the mall a few weeks prior who seemed to adore me, however. The last time Chester and I saw each other he told me he wanted to take me to Las Vegas. Chester and I weren't in an exclusive relationship and, in fact, hadn't even kissed yet. Unlike Trenton, Chester had a small frame, wore black framed, circular glasses, and dressed in khakis, polos, and button down shirts. He worked as an accountant for a big corporation in town, and often bragged about how much money he had, and as a result he could take care of me. Chester would be classified as a square, while Trenton had swag, which is what I ultimately preferred. But Chester was kind, and although I had known him only a short time, I was intrigued because he was so into me. I knew, however, I wasn't physically attracted to him, and didn't think that would change.

On the side of the highway, during the ten minutes we spoke, I discovered Trenton transported goods across the country for work. He was headed to Detroit from his hometown of LA for this trip. This was a route he often took. He was single, had no children, and was looking to settle down. He was also ten years my senior.

As he spoke I was in a trance by how handsome he was. Up close his skin was flawless, almost dewy. And his teeth were straight and super white. A beautiful smile was my weakness.

We exchanged numbers, hugged, and off we went. I didn't ask when he would call me because I didn't want to seem desperate, but I hoped he would reach out later that day. It would be three days before I heard from him.

From the moment Haily and Jaari saw each other, they couldn't keep their hands off one another. I was happy for her. I longed for a love like this.

I would catch Jaari staring at me, but acted as if that wasn't happening. I really wanted whatever he and Hailey had to withstand the test of time. The next day when Hailey was in the shower, Jaari approached me about what he was feeling for me. He asked if I was feeling the same way. I told him I felt it too, but that he was with Hailey so we should let things be. Although I felt uncomfortable about the situation, I figured that we would leave the conversation there. I never told Hailey because I didn't want to disrupt what she and Jaari had. Plus I didn't know how she would react to this. Hailey was already deeply insecure, and I didn't want to feed into her insecurity and put myself at jeopardy of not having a place to live since it was technically her apartment. My name hadn't been added to the lease when I moved in so by default I was a guest in the home where I was paying rent.

Trenton and I continued to talk for weeks. I learned he was originally from Oakland, California and he had a trade business that forced him to travel from coast to coast. The details were fuzzy about what exactly this entailed. I tried tenaciously to get more details, but I was always left feeling unclear about what he actually did. I decided not to push too hard though. I really liked him and didn't want to do anything to turn him off.

The more we spoke, the more adamant he became about me coming to see him. There was a part of me that really wanted to, but there was another part of me that felt something was off about him so I never committed to going. For some reason though, I felt a sense of comfort with sharing intimate details of my life. I told him about the strained relationship with my father and that he opted not to go to my high school graduation to attend my brother Daquan's baseball game. I told him about the relationship dynamics with my mother. I even told him about the time I had been locked up. The more we talked the more I wanted him to know everything about me.

We spoke every couple days and then one day he called and told me he was in town and wanted to come see me. I was surprised that he just showed up all the way from California without telling me he was coming into town. I didn't feel at ease with him coming to our apartment. I really wanted to see him though, so I told him I'd meet him at the mall.

As I rode to the mall, it dawned on me that I had given him so much information about me, but knew very little about him. When he saw me he had this sly look on his face which, for the first time, made me a little uneasy. I still chose to embrace him upon entering his space. There were two men with him that he introduced as Tye and Shawn. Once we sat down, they hung back not too far from where we were.

"Hey, baby, you look good!"

"Thanks—you're not too bad yourself. Nearly dressed exactly the same as you were last time. This must be your signature style."

"You know it. I know what I like. And I'm really feeling you."

"What are you feeling about me?"

"I just like you."

"What do you like about me?"

"Girl, you're on that question train today, huh?"

"I'm just curious."

"I like how you look, that's for sure."

"That's sweet—what else?"

"What else is there?"

"I mean there is a lot more than looks. I've told you a lot about me."

"Yeah."

"So you don't have an answer to that question?"

"Let me think about it. I just want to enjoy you right now. Damn, you're eye candy!"

"Again, I appreciate that, and I really want to know."

"I made it a point to stop here to see you. Doesn't that count for something?"

"Sure it does. I'm glad you're here. It's good to see you."

"So why are you sweating me with all these questions then?"

"I would just think that you could tell me what you like about me, especially because you want me to come to California."

"I do want you to come. I'll get you a ticket right now, in fact, you could just ride back with us."

"I've got school, work. I can't just get up and leave with you right now."

"You work at the ice cream shop and you don't need school. I'll take care of you. Money is nothing to me. I have lots of it."

"I can see that. I appreciate you wanting to take care of me, but we haven't known each other that long. And honestly I don't need anyone to take care of me."

"I'm trying to give you a lifestyle that you can only dream of. Don't you want that?"

For a moment I considered Trenton's proposition. I had taken care of myself for the last seven years and scraped by to get the clothes I wanted or pay my rent. What was so wrong with allowing someone to take care of me? But I didn't know if that's what I wanted for my life. And what would I do in California alone—with no friends or family?

"I mean it sounds good, but we're still getting to know each other.

Perhaps we can go slower and maybe we can revisit this once we have a better sense of each other."

"Revisit it? You don't even know the kind of life I could give to you girl."

"I have a sense. I saw your car, how you dress. It's clear you have money."

"Don't you want that? I'm quite generous. We could even go shopping right now so you can get a taste of what life would be like with me in Cali."

"I'm good. We can just keep talking here."

"You're tripping. What kind of woman would reject a proposition like this, and from a man like me?"

"There's a first time for everything."

"I guess so."

I could tell he was agitated. He walked over to Tye and Shawn, they exchanged a few words, and when he came back he said they had a call come in and needed to do a pick-up.

"So soon, huh? You haven't even been here fifteen minutes."

"Yeah that's the way it is. When business calls, business calls."

"What do you have to pick up?"

"A package."

"What kind of package?"

"There you go again with the questions."

"This seems like a pretty simple one. I'm trying to understand what you do."

"All you need to know is what I do makes me a lot of money. You don't need to know the details. Just know I have enough to take care of you. That's all you need to worry about."

Before I could respond he got up to leave and asked for a hug before they headed out the mall.

"I'll call you."

"When?"

"When I do. Soon."

A whole week would go by before I heard from Trenton. I wanted to know why he had taken so long to reach out. He explained he had been busy and didn't like being questioned, yet again.

"You seem upset."

"Honestly, I am."

"Why? I'm simply trying to get to know you, understand you."

"There isn't much to know or understand."

"I don't agree with that. I think there is much to get to know about a person. I'm still not clear about exactly what you do, for example."

"I already told you. What I do is make deliveries. I make money. What else is there to know?"

"What are you delivering?"

"I'm not sure how many times you're going to ask me this. I'm not going to give you a different answer than I already have."

"I just don't understand why your work is such a secret."

There was silence for a long time before he changed the subject and inquired, once again, about me coming to California. I shared that

I wasn't comfortable visiting someone that I knew so little about. His tone softened. He said he understood and he would wait for me because I was worth waiting for. Another call came in on his line, and when he returned he said he had to go but he'd reach out again soon. I never heard from him again.

Meanwhile Chester started coming around more, and I finally agreed to go to Las Vegas with him. My physical attraction to Chester hadn't changed but I liked that he was consistent and did things that made me feel special like coming to visit me at work, sending me flowers, and now this trip to Vegas. By the time we left, we had only kissed once, had never held hands, and when he would attempt to be physical with me I pulled away except the one day I gave in and kissed him. I didn't like how I felt when we kissed but I never articulated this to Chester. I also didn't tell him that I wasn't attracted to him and therefore didn't see a future for us.

We stayed at the Luxor, shopped, went to a show, gambled a little, ate at some great restaurants, and walked the strip. One day when we were shopping we even saw Babyface having lunch. I was grateful Chester hadn't come on to me because although he had been patient with my boundaries I didn't know how he'd feel now after spending all this time and money on me.

We stayed in the same room with two full beds. I insisted on sleeping by myself which he seemed okay with until the last night before we headed back to Michigan.

Chester climbed into bed with me after I repeatedly asked him not to. He became aggressive and told me that he had been patient enough and it was time. I told him I didn't want to have sex, wasn't comfortable with it, and he became irate. He got on top of me, and placed his hand over my wrists which wouldn't have mattered because I already couldn't move. All I could manage to do is repeat over and over again that I didn't want this through my tears.

Chester sat on my pelvis, knelt over my chest and just stared at me, never uttering a word. After a few minutes, he got up and stood near the bed all while continuing to gaze at me in silence. My tears continued to flow while my body was still immobile, but I could see him out of the corner of my eye. I wondered what he was thinking, but I dared not ask. Eventually he got in the other bed. And somehow I managed to cry myself to sleep.

There was silence between us the next morning that carried through packing, breakfast, the cab ride to the airport, the airport, the plane ride, and the car ride home. When I arrived back home I knew I would never talk to Chester again. I was ashamed that I had once again put myself in a situation where I could have been harmed, but I was grateful for the divine protection at the same time. When we arrived at my building, I got out of the car and collected my belongings as fast as I could. Neither one of us said a word to each other. When I turned around Chester was long gone. I was relieved that it was over. As soon as I got to the safety of my room, the tears came again. And they didn't stop until the next morning.

That weekend Hailey and I went to our friend Kathy's house for a get together because Jaari had come to town to visit. After a few hours of drinking and smoking weed, Jaari approached me as I came out of the bathroom, wanting to revisit the conversation we last had. I tried to shut him down and quickly move back to the space where everyone was but he wouldn't allow me to go past him. Before I could escape, Hailey approached and asked what was going on. Jaari lied and said I had come on to him. That sent Hailey into a frenzy.

I couldn't believe how quickly she sided with him. That day I discovered that in matters of the heart, people are sometimes irrational. I had been attracted to him, but resisted the urge to do anything about my attraction. However, I found myself in a situation where I was made to be the villain with absolutely no benefit of the doubt. The next day I moved out of Hailey's apartment and back home until I could scrape up enough cash to move out on my own for good.

Chapter 10

Desperately Searching

Malachi had a crush on me for as long as I could remember. We had been friends for years. I was never particularly interested in him, but he had always been a perfect gentleman. After leaving the dry cleaners to work at Kalamazoo Advantage Academy, my life slowly started to change. I left drugs behind, except for marijuana, and drinking had mostly dissipated as well.

On the first day at the academy I met Jala who I started attending church with. Church wasn't something new to me. I had been attending church since I was a little girl. My grandmother had been raised Catholic and even thought about becoming a nun after attending Catholic boarding school. By the time I was born, she and my mother had taken on a nondenominational faith. This resulted in us attending church regularly which, as a child, I thoroughly enjoyed. I was even active in the puppet ministry until middle school, when I mostly stopped attending church.

Even when I would go, I had become such a drifter I would sometimes attend while I was high. One time I stayed up all night doing meth. My mother kept hounding me about my dilated pupils that day, but I remained steadfast that nothing was wrong with me, and I was simply tired.

Faith was not very far from me, however. Every time I'd see my grandmother she'd say, *"I'm keeping you in that Psalm 91,"* which was her way of saying she was praying for me, and that I was divinely protected. Although I didn't feel protected, her words soothed me.

Jala attended a church where, at most, there would be twenty people in attendance. The pastor rented space at a community center which could easily accommodate the small number of people who would gather each Sunday–including his three children and his wife. It was here that I found solace, and started to regain my faith in God. It was also here that I found the foundation for a better life for myself.

Equipped with my renewed faith, I decided that I would give Malachi a try, however whenever he tried to be intimate with me I couldn't bring myself to reciprocate. So when he asked me to marry him–only a few months into dating, I was shocked. But what I was more shocked by was that I said yes, as if I really meant it.

Malachi represented a pathway to a better life for me. He had a stable job and a nice car. He adored his mother. And I never witnessed him being disrespectful to women. Yet, I couldn't bring myself to tell anyone about our engagement. I also made it clear to Malachi that I wasn't really interested in having sex and desired to take things super slow. He seemed perfectly okay with this and never pushed me, although he was persistent in his desire for physical intimacy.

Living with Kendall, a friend of my grandmother's, and someone I worked with at the academy, was a breath of fresh air. After a few weeks at the academy, she offered to let me rent the empty bedroom in her home after she discovered that I had been looking to move out of my mom's. She had known my grandmother for years after attending the same church and working as lead teacher at Chikere's day care. We met a few years prior when I was working with infants and toddlers, which I loved. When I was younger I thought for sure I'd be a pediatrician but by the time I was thirteen that dream had fallen away. My love for children, on the other hand, never diminished, so when I was given the opportunity to work for the academy I jumped.

I adored Kendall's kids, Mason & Riley. We would start the day by jamming out to music and the phrase, *"This is my jam,"* that I frequently used, became synonymous with the kids. Kendall's husband Jack was pleasant but mainly kept to himself. I'd come home from work and he'd always be in the same spot in the kitchen drinking dark liquor. That's exactly where Mason found him after school one day, immersed in blood from a gunshot wound to the head. It was well-known by everyone that he had been depressed for years but after he lost his job he spiraled downward quickly, although nothing could have prepared the family for suicide.

It became increasingly hard for me to maintain an inner peace at Kendall's after Jack's death, so when Malachi asked me to go to New York with him I agreed. His aunt lived in the Bronx and was whom we would stay with. We'd leave for winter break since I had two weeks paid time off at that point. That was one of the things I loved about working at the academy—all the paid time off I received. Not to mention, of course, working with adolescents brought me immense joy.

So Malachi and I were off for a road trip to NYC while his closest friend, Bem, and girlfriend, Laqueta, followed. I had hung out with them on a few occasions and quickly realized they had an open relationship which was something I had just been introduced to. One night when we were playing cards, they kept alluding to this and clearly wanted to have a sexual experience with Malachi and me. I made it clear I wanted nothing to do with this and not just because Malachi and I hadn't been intimate yet. Honestly, it scared me.

The Bronx was nothing like I had imagined. His aunt lived in an apartment building that had at least 300 apartments in it. I don't think I had ever seen a building that big in my life. When we walked inside there was a feeling of warmth. I was glad about this. Malachi's aunt hugged me so tightly and welcomed me with, *"Hey, baby! Malachi has told me so much about you!"* This made me feel at ease and yet slightly uncomfortable at the same time. I wondered if "so much" included the engagement or just that we were seeing each other. The pressure of having to talk about the engagement and my feelings for Malachi overwhelmed me.

That evening Malachi slept on the floor, I slept on the sofa bed, and Bem & Laqueta slept on the larger couch. The next day I woke up, showered, and eagerly waited for what the day would bring. After breakfast we headed over to Malachi's friend's house who lived in the same complex. I was attracted to Rick instantly, but I tried to resist this attraction. I could tell he was attracted to me, too. I wondered if

Malachi had picked up on this. Later that day, when Malachi was running errands, he told me it was okay to hang out at Rick's until he got back. We innocently flirted. Outside of that, no lines were crossed, although I still felt guilty.

When Malachi returned, he picked me up from Rick's and informed me we were going into the city today, meaning Manhattan. He talked about Manhattan like it was the best place in the world. I could hardly wait. I had done a little research prior to leaving for our trip so I knew exactly where I wanted to go. When I shared this with Malachi I discovered that my plan countered his plans. We bickered for thirty minutes as we drove into the city, although I didn't allow it to deter me from taking in the scenery. I had never witnessed such beauty. Crossing the Brooklyn Bridge, seeing the Statue of Liberty from afar, the architecture, the skyline. I was in love with New York.

Later we went to Malachi's favorite restaurant called *Jamaican Sweets & Treats* that was right outside of Manhattan. After we ate, he dropped me off at Macy's on 34th St. We agreed on a time that he would pick me up, along with a location, and he drove off.

I explored every aisle on every floor that had anything that looked remotely like it was for women. After finding a few items I liked, I looked down at my watch and realized it was fifteen minutes past the time Malachi was scheduled to pick me up. I was on the top floor of the store. I calculated another five minutes before I could get outside to my destination. Once outside there was no Malachi. I figured he had been running late or maybe he had come and was driving around the block to kill some time. After thirty minutes of waiting, it became completely dark. After another fifteen minutes, Macy's and most stores in the vicinity, had closed for the evening. It was now 9 o'clock. Panic set in as I wondered what the hell I would do. I didn't have the address of where we were staying. I didn't even have a phone number to call anyone, or the last name of his aunt to look her up. I didn't even know the name of the apartment complex where I was staying.

Luckily, I did have money on me. I thought about walking to the subway station to see if I could figure out a way to get back to the Bronx. The only problem was I didn't know where the station was and I was too afraid to ask anyone on the street. Being a young woman in the streets of Manhattan carrying shopping bags from Macy's terrified me. Instead I thought it best to act like I was a New Yorker. I figured I would walk until I found something that looked like a subway station. After walking for about an hour, I stumbled onto a cab driver and asked him to take me to the Bronx. I told him that I didn't know the exact name of where I was going but described many things in the area to try and help him pinpoint a location. I somehow managed to remember the street name too. The cab driver nodded indicating to me he knew where to take me, but when we reached the destination it was a dark alley instead.

"Sir, this is not where my stop is."

"Yes, you told me Biggs St., in the Bronx. This is where we are."

"Yes, sir. I see that, but this is not my destination."

"Well this is what you told me."

"I know what I told you but this is not my stop. I can't get out here. I am alone with two shopping bags. That can't be safe."

"My shift is ending. I will take you back to the station. Maybe someone can help us there."

What choice did I have? I could roam the streets of wherever I was, or I could try to figure out where I was going. As I sat in the back of the cab, I remembered my grandmother's words, *"I keep you in that Psalm 91."* I prayed for safety, and that I would find my way back.

I was relieved when we arrived at the cab company. There was a Jamaican man sitting at the desk. I tried to describe where I was going, and he was clueless. He continued to tell me to wait a moment and he would call some of his drivers who may know based on the description. He indicated that there was one who might know, but I would have to wait for him to dispatch. I kept my eyes on the clock the entire time, clenched my purse by my side and kept my bags tightly between my legs. Each time the clock would change, it would make me that much more uneasy. Twenty minutes had passed. By the time the cab driver called in it was 11:22 p.m.

"Sir, do you know what time the driver will be here?"

"No, maam, but I do know he is on his way. Just relax. He should be here momentarily."

I couldn't relax no matter how hard I tried. And my thoughts started to race.

Had Malachi left me on purpose?

Why did I have to be late?

Why did I leave them in the first place?

Why didn't I know where I was going?

How could I be so stupid?

What the fuck was wrong with me?

I knew nothing about the city of New York. I hadn't even traveled outside of Michigan since I was a little girl except for my escapade to Las Vegas. I was so naive. How could I leave anywhere with no address, no phone number. I was so angry with myself that I almost started to cry right there in the cab station with the two men I had just met. It took everything for me to hold back my tears. I knew it would have been a sign of weakness and I had too many things stacked against me already. Holding back my tears was one thing I could control.

I looked at the clock again and another seventeen minutes had passed. I decided that I would wait until 11:45 p.m. and, if no one came by that time, I would just start walking. When it was 11:45 p.m. I got up, thanked the Jamaican for his time, and informed him I couldn't wait any longer. He advised me that walking on the streets alone at night could be dangerous for someone like me, but I didn't listen. I appreciated that he was trying to look out for me but I couldn't just sit here while the time passed. I needed to figure out a way to get back to Malachi. He had to be–at least I hoped he was– worried sick by now. On my way out the door the Jamaican gave me some tips that would help me blend in. The only problem was I knew

I didn't blend in with these two large Macy's bags. I started to leave the bags behind, but thought that if I did that I would probably never see them again.

I walked quickly and avoided eye contact with anyone on the street. With the exception of a few cat calls, no one seemed to bother me. I ended up on what looked like the main street the Jamaican told me about. I was relieved to be on a well-lit street with businesses open–even if they were liquor stores. I went into the first liquor store I saw, purchased a bottle of water, and attempted to describe to the man at the register where I was headed. He said he was sorry but he couldn't assist me. As soon as I left the store a red Honda Civic approached me and asked if I needed a ride. I described to him where I was going and he acted like he knew exactly what I had described. Relieved, I got in his car and we sped off.

"I'm Jose."

"Hi. I'm Demarra."

"Apparently you're not from here."

"Obvious, huh?"

"Yeah. And how you gonna be out here like that and not know where you are staying, or how to get in touch with the people you're staying with?"

"I know. It was stupid. I was with some friends in downtown Manhattan. They were supposed to pick me up in front of Macy's at 8 p.m. and they weren't there."

"Damn girl, that's cold!"

"I was about twenty minutes late though, so I am hoping they came and left thinking I had ditched them or something."

"Yeah but they shouldn't have left you all alone. Especially not in a city like New York."

"I agree. But like I said I would prefer to think I left them."

"That's cool. So where are you staying?"

"In the Bronx."

"Where in the Bronx?"

"I'm not sure exactly. It is on Biggs St. near a McDonalds. The complex is huge. Do you know which one I am talking about?"

"I know the Bronx pretty well. Based on the description you gave you're talking about the Croydens. Does that sound familiar?"

"Vaguely. If the complex you are referring to is on the street I said near a McDonalds then yes, that's the one."\

"You don't have a phone number or a name so we can look the number up? We can call them on my cell phone."

"No, I don't. I guess I never imagined I would be separated from them."

"I hear you, but you should never rely on others. Anything could happen, just like it did tonight. You just happened to be in the right place at the right time. What would you have done if I hadn't stopped my car and asked if you needed a ride?"

"I really don't know."

"It is what it is. It's still pretty early. Do you want to hang out for a little while before I take you back?"

"It's going on 1 a.m. You call that early?"

"In New York we party all night, so yeah, for most of us at 1 a.m. things are just getting started."

"I should probably get back. I can imagine how worried my friends must be."

"We'll only stay out for a couple more hours. I'll have you back in no time. We can go to this bar and have a few drinks not far from here."

I hesitated, but then gave in. I could use a drink after the kind of day I had. Plus Jose had been so kind, the least I could do was hang out with him for a few hours.

"Sure, why not? They've waited this long. What's a couple more hours?"

We sped off and headed to the bar. I discovered that Jose was a hairdresser who just so happened to cut the hair of a famous Latino rapper. He claimed he and Fat Joe had grown up together and, even though he had superstar status, he was just Fat Joe to everyone in the neighborhood. I thought that was so cool. I had never met anyone who had close contact with a superstar. We arrived at the bar and ordered drinks. I ordered a Long Island iced tea while he ordered a Heineken. Without even realizing it I drank half of my first drink in one gulp.

"Damn, girl. Slow down. We got time. I'll buy you as many of those as you want. Nurse your drink a little. That way I'll have more time with you."

We continued to engage in conversation as we sat and drank. He kept telling me how beautiful I was and if he had someone like me he would never leave them. I was flattered, so I flirted to be nice. After my third drink I was feeling pretty good. I got up to go to the bathroom, but stumbled and trampled over my two feet instead. Jose helped me up, walked me to the bathroom, and waited for me until I was done. When I returned he suggested it was probably time to go.

"But as you said we just got here," I slurred.

"Yeah, but I think you've had enough. You can barely stand up."

I laughed. "You're probably right. Let's go!"

He walked me to the car and opened the door for me. I must have nodded off in the car because when the car stopped I realized I was in an area that wasn't familiar to me. The car door opened and Jose helped me out of the car.

"Where are we?"

"We're at my apartment."

"I thought you were going to take me back to my friends."

"I am, but I thought you could sober up a little before I take you back."

"What time is it?"

"2:30 a.m."

"You're still going to take me back in about an hour right?"

"Sure. I keep my word."

"Okay."

We headed upstairs to his apartment. It was small, but everything seemed to be in its place. He asked if I wanted another drink once I was settled on the couch in the living room.

"I thought the whole purpose of me coming to your apartment was to sober up, not get more drunk than I am right now."

"I wouldn't be hospitable if I didn't offer. What about some water?"

"Yes, water would be great."

I must have dozed off or blacked out because I woke up to find Jose on top of me. This was an unpleasant surprise.

"What are you doing?"

"What do you mean, what am I doing, we're having sex."

"I know we're having sex, but I don't even remember going from the couch to the bed."

"Oh, well, we started kissing and before I knew it you had taken off your shirt. I just assumed you wanted to have sex. You still want to have sex, right?"

I felt bad. I knew he was probably telling the truth. This wasn't the first time I blacked out and found myself somewhere I hadn't planned on being. It was embarrassing. More importantly it was dangerous.

"Sure. You have a condom on right?"

"Of course. I always wear one. You never know these days–no offense."

I was relieved that at least he was wearing protection. I certainly didn't want to find myself with another STD or worse, HIV. Before he could finish we realized my period started.

"What the fuck?!?!? Girl you just bled all over my sheets."

"I'm so sorry my cycle must have started."

"You could have warned me."

"How the hell was I supposed to know my period was going to start?"

"It's about time I take you to your friends."

"Let me change your sheets before I leave."

"I think you've done enough. It's time to go."

I was too embarrassed to argue so instead I scurried around the house to find my clothes and got dressed as quickly as I could. On the twenty minute ride to my destination there was nothing but silence. As we approached the highrise, I felt peace. I told Jose how appreciative I was and again apologized for the sheets. He accepted both my apology and gratitude. We said goodbye, and just as fast as he came into my life, he was gone.

I watched the red Honda Civic hatchback take off. Once the car was gone I plopped down on the steps and reflected on all that had happened. I was mortified that I had just slept with someone I knew nothing about and wouldn't even kiss the man who had brought me thousands of miles from where I lived to be with his family. Not to mention, I had been crushing on his best friend. *What was wrong with me?*

I looked down at my watch to discover it was almost 4 a.m. I was still hazy from the three Long Islands I had just a while before. I did my best to steady myself and fix my disheveled state, but it was no use. I knew Malachi would have a lot of questions that I wasn't prepared to answer. Fear sank in as I rang the buzzer.

Once I was granted access, I stumbled into the building, off the elevator, and towards the apartment. Malachi must have heard my footsteps because before I made it to the door, he came into the hallway. He watched me as I made my way into the apartment but spoke no words. When I was within a foot of him all he said was, *"Where the hell have you been?"*

His tone startled me. I had never heard Malachi speak to anyone in that manner. I had expected some form of relief that I had made it back, but instead, all I got was anger.

"Where were you?"

"I came out of Macy's and you were gone. I waited for a while and thought you had left me. Maybe you were upset that we were fighting."

"Don't try to play me, Demarra. We came to get you at 8 p.m. The time we agreed upon, but you were nowhere in sight. I have been looking for you for hours. Where the fuck have you been? Plus, you're drunk. I saw how you were stumbling. And you smell like a distillery."

"Malachi, I'm not trying to play you. I was a little late coming out. I was mesmerized by all the things they had in the store and lost track of time. When I looked at my watch it read 8:05 p.m. and I hadn't even checked out yet. I told the clerk I needed to hurry so I wouldn't miss my ride. As you know, I had no way of calling you to tell you I would be late. I then rushed downstairs but by the time I made it there it was twenty after. I waited there for about forty minutes before I decided I would try to get back here somehow. I didn't have an address. I didn't even remember the name of the complex. All I could remember was that I was in the Bronx, the name of the main street, and that the building was near a McDonalds."

"Who the fuck goes somewhere and doesn't have an address or a name of the building where they're staying? How could you be so fucking stupid?"

"You're right. I don't know why I didn't think to have that kind of information with me. I guess I was too reliant on you. I never thought I would be separated from you."

"Well, that's exactly what happened to your stupid ass isn't it? You need to call your mom. She is worried sick about you."

"You called my mom?"

"Hell yeah I called her. I didn't know what to do. We thought you had been abducted or something. Naw, I shoulda known better. Your ass was off drinking somewhere and I bet with some dude, wasn't it? Don't even answer that question right now. Just call your mom! We'll finish our conversation as soon as you get off the phone with her."

I felt so confined in that little apartment. I preferred to talk with her in private, but I didn't have the audacity to request this.

"Hey, mom."

"Hey, honey. Are you okay?"

"Yes, I'm fine."

"What happened?"

"I was late getting to the destination where Malachi said he would pick me up and they left thinking that I left them. I waited another forty minutes or so before I started walking to try to find someone who could help me get back here."

"You didn't have a way to contact anyone? Why didn't you call me? We were all worried sick about you. I thought I was going to have to fly out there tomorrow to help look for you."

"I didn't. I know I should have had a number, a name, an address, but I didn't. Lesson learned."

"Okay, I'm just glad you're safe. Let's pray."

As my mother recited Psalm 91, I felt solace. I wanted to hold on to that feeling, It was the most comfortable I had felt since coming to New York. I knew enough to know that feeling would go away instantly after I got off the phone with her, but I was grateful I had it for the moment. When she was done saying the prayer I longed to keep talking to her, but it was time. I didn't want to face Malachi's rage.

"Love you, Demarra."

"I love you too, mom."

For a few seconds after I hung up, my head hung low, and my body seemed to sink in the chair as I sat with my racing thoughts. Malachi approached me and said we should go outside to talk so I obliged. On the way down we didn't exchange words. Once off the elevator, Rick greeted us but didn't acknowledge my presence at all.

When we got outside the building, Malachi and Rick walked towards the parking lot as I trailed behind. I was confused considering Malachi said we were going outside to talk. I stopped before stepping off the sidewalk and inquired about where we were headed.

"Where the hell do you think we're headed? Can't you see I'm going to the car?"

"Yes, I can see that, but why? I thought we were just going to sit on the curb and talk. And alone. Why is Rick here?"

"Because I want him to be here. You thought wrong. Now get your ass in the car, before you piss me off even more than I am right now."

"I understand that you're upset with me. I just want to know where we're going at this time of morning."

"Dude, you hear this? Can you believe this chick? Oh, so now you're concerned with the time. You weren't concerned with the time when you were out galavanting on the streets of New York, were you? Demarra, I'm not going to say it again. Get your ass in the car. You can get in using your free will, or I can force your ass in. I'm assuming you would prefer the first option."

I got in the car. This side of him made me uneasy. Up until this point, I could anticipate his every move, but now I was clueless about what he was going to do. I sat in silence while Malachi and Rick bantered back and forth. Malachi rolled a blunt and he and Rick started to partake, but didn't offer me any, although I had no desire to smoke. I needed to be as alert as I could. A couple minutes later the

174

car was filled entirely with smoke, and then Malachi turned to me to try to get me to indulge.

"You want some?"

"No. I'm fine."

"What do you mean you're fine? Girl you better take a hit of this weed."

"Malachi, I'm good."

"As long as I've known you, you have never turned down some ganja."

"I'm tired. That's all."

"Yeah, we're all fucking tired. We have been waiting on your ass all night, remember? But you see it hasn't stopped me from smoking. Oh, I know what it is, look at you, your ass is pissy drunk."

"Malachi, I just don't feel well. That's all."

"Oh, you don't feel well? That's because you're a snake. You wander off in New York to go off with some dude and get inebriated. You probably fucked him, didn't you? How are you gonna play me like this? I brought your ass all the way here and you embarrass me like this in front of my family? My friends? Who the fuck do you think you are? You think you can trample all over people and they will simply allow you to do that shit? You got the wrong dude if you think that's what I'm about."

Although I had slept with Jose, there was no way I was going to tell Malachi that. If I hadn't been drinking I would never have done it. But the fact was, I did. And I felt horrible for doing so. I didn't know what he would do to me if he knew that part of the story.

"Malachi, I swear it's not like that. Just give me a chance to tell you what happened."

"Oh, you want a chance to tell me what happened? I don't need to know shit about what happened to you. You want to know why? Because I'm not going to believe a goddamn word out of your mouth. I should have never hooked up with you. You are a user. Yep, that's what you are! I'm a good mutha fucking man and this is how you treat me? Women always talk about wanting a good man, but naw, y'all hoes don't want that. When you get a good man you don't know a damn thing about how to treat them."

"If you would please let me tell you what happened then you would understand that I'm not the person you think I am."

"I know exactly what kind of person you are. Not only are you the kind of person that uses people. You are also the kind of person who would go behind her man's back and do something as dirty as try to get with my boy."

I was speechless. I had no idea what Rick had told Malachi, but it didn't matter considering they had been friends for years, and it was clear my words meant nothing anymore.

"Your ass doesn't have anything to say now, do you? You know I should kill you. Throw your ass in a body of water somewhere. I could choke you right now. It would be so easy. You'd be dead in a matter of seconds. We're in this car. No one would hear you scream. Everyone is sleeping by now at the house. Go on and look up there.

See the windows. Totally pitch black. They wouldn't even know I left the parking lot. You ran off once. If you ran off again no one would be surprised."

I couldn't believe the words coming out of Malachi's mouth. I knew he was angry, but nothing could have prepared me for this kind of rage. I started to cry. I felt helpless. I was alone.

"Look at this! Can you believe this? She's got the nerve to be crying after the shit she pulled. You think I feel bad about you crying? Well I don't. In fact, it is infuriating to me. Shut the fuck up! I can't think with all this crying!"

Rick chimed in, "Man, be cool. Ain't no chick worth you losing your cool like this."

"So, you sticking up for her?"

"Naw man, I'm just saying she ain't worth it. You up in here talking about killing and shit. That's not the Malachi I grew up with. Think about it! You just heated right now. You don't really mean what you're saying."

"You must be saying all this because you like her."

"She's cool, but what I just spit at you has nothing to do with her. You talking crazy, man. I'm just trying to prevent you from doing something stupid you might regret."

"True. Man, that was crazy wasn't it?!? I'm sitting here talking about killing and shit. That ain't even me. See what no good bitches bring out of you?"

Then Malachi turned to me and stared for a while before uttering

177

another word. My head hung low but I could feel the intensity of his energy.

"I'm telling you right now, you better be happy that Rick spoke some sense into me because your ass was about to be done with. From here on out you and me are through. I don't give a fuck what you do."

"Malachi, can't we talk about this?'"

"Naw, there is nothing to talk about. I said all that I had to say about the situation. I'm not going to throw your ass on the streets because where the fuck would you go? But you're on your own with getting home. There is no way in hell I'm riding in the car with you."

"So, how am I going to get home?"

"That's your problem. Not mine. You'll figure it out."

"But, Malachi . . ."

"Look, Demarra, I'm warning you not to push the issue. I won't change my mind. Plus, I don't want to keep rehashing this shit. I'll go my way and you'll go yours."

Not only had an engagement ended, but years of friendship had been destroyed in one day. The next day was New Year's Eve and although Malachi and I had made plans to see the ball drop together, I knew that wasn't going to happen, so when Bem, Laqueta, and Malachi headed out with no regard for me, I wasn't surprised.

I longed for the comfort of home. I didn't want to burden my mother with what had just happened with Malachi and me. For all she knew I was safe, and that's what mattered. Plus I knew her finances were tight, so asking her for the money to fly home wasn't an option. I hoped that Laqueta and Bem would allow me to ride home with them. Laqueta had already been skeptical of me because of the amount of attention Bem focused on me when we were all together. I knew this was why she never particularly warmed to me. Now that Malachi and I weren't together there was no longer a perceived protective shield around me. I was just out there in the universe alone and single.

I woke up to find that Bem and Laqueta were already up and packing. I greeted both of them, but only Bem responded. This would be my only chance to get home so, although I knew Laqueta wanted nothing to do with me, I asked if they would be kind enough to allow me to ride home with them. Laqueta said the car was too packed and there wouldn't be anywhere for me to sit. Bem said they would make it work but it would be tight. Laqueta kept going on but Bem made it clear that they could manage, although the ride might be uncomfortable for me. She agreed but only if I covered the cost of gas on the way home. I happily obliged. Although I only had $100 left, I figured that would be enough. It didn't matter if the cost of gas ate up every dollar I had as long as I made it home.

Once we were done loading, there was only enough room for the width of my body on the seat, which meant my hips and legs were sandwiched tightly between their luggage and the car door. I carried my luggage on my lap. Sleep was impossible in the cramped back seat so the only form of respite I received was when we stopped to eat, use the restroom, or get gas. Every time we would stop, Laqueta would take the cash without saying thank you and no matter the cost she would never bring me my change. She knew I was in a powerless position and she took every advantage of it. Nevertheless I was thankful to have a ride home and counted my blessings.

A snow storm started to approach that morning. The roads were covered in snow and black ice which nearly swallowed the tiny blue Hyundai we rode in. We almost drove off the road on numerous occasions. I prayed more on our way back than I had probably in my entire life. When we finally turned onto my street I beamed with joy. The only words I had were, *"Thank you, God."*

I repeated this to myself over and over again until we pulled in the driveway, as I walked up to the door, and for several minutes after I entered the warmth of Kendall's. I hugged her and the kids as if my dear life depended on it. They had so many questions about my trip and although I wanted to answer them all, I knew at that moment I didn't have it in me. Instead, I requested a long nap and told them I would tell them all the details once I woke up. As I brought my luggage up to my room, and plopped down on the bed, I was overtaken by my emotions. All I could ponder was what I had just survived. Before I went to bed, I took the longest bath of my life and then slept for what felt like days. Nearly twenty-four hours to be exact.

A few days later, on Sunday, I agreed to go to church with my mother. When the pastor called people up for prayer I was one of the first to go. I knew I no longer wanted to live the way I had been living or be the person I had become. I desperately wanted change, and it was up to me to make it happen. When the prayer started I broke down in tears allowing gravity to pull me to my knees as I raised my hands to surrender to all that was. As I walked back to my seat I had a feeling that I would never be the same.

THE PIVOT TO LIBERATION

Chapter 11
15 Years of Solace

About a year later, I finally settled on getting a degree in elementary education with an emphasis in early childhood. I had been with the academy for a year which I absolutely loved. My relationship with spirituality started to deepen as a result of attending church weekly and spending more and more time with Jala. I even started to bring my friends with me during the rare times they would hesitantly agree.

Right before my nineteenth birthday, I went out with Tessa so we could celebrate her nineteenth birthday which was exactly one week before mine. On our way to The Nuvo Room, Tessa ran into a guy she was seeing named Bast. Right next to Bast there he was a tall, milk chocolate, lean man with a semi-thick black mustache and magnetic smile named Curtis. His fade had deep waves and he was dressed in dark blue jeans and a black tank top that showed off his muscular arms. He was cute, but his smile, more than anything, caught my attention. Eventually he asked for my phone number and I started to grill him about his motives, making it clear I had no intention of having sex with him. He never called.

The following week was my birthday and I went back to the same place. On my way out of the bathroom, I ran into Curtis. I instantly confronted him about not calling. He desperately tried to get away from me but I wouldn't let him. I wanted answers. About an hour later we were on the dance floor and stayed there until the club closed. Then we headed to Steak & Shake, where he had a double bacon cheeseburger and a strawberry shake and I had a patty melt with a chocolate shake as we talked for hours. When we got back to my place, he walked me to the door, kissed me, and went on his way. For the six weeks that followed we were pretty much inseparable. When Sweetest Day rolled around, he had a half dozen pink roses sent to the academy. For the first time I started to understand what love could look like between two people.

Although there were many things I loved about Curtis, like how he treated the women in his family, how he listened to me, kept me laughing, and the quiet sense of surety he had about himself, when he wanted to make things official, it scared me. I didn't know if I was ready to be firmly committed to someone else. We seemed to be that without the formalization. Proclaiming I was all in wasn't something I felt I could do, so instead I asked to be friends. And that's what we were until about a year later when we realized there was no one else for either of us.

Our courtship lasted about nine months before he asked me to marry him. A few months later I obtained my associate's degree from Kalamazoo Community College and headed to Western Michigan University to obtain my bachelor's degree.

When we announced our engagement to our families they weren't particularly thrilled. My family wasn't overt with their feelings around the both of us, although my mother had many private conversations with me about how out of alignment she felt the two of us were long-term. His family, on the other hand, made it known through the way they treated me that I was simply not suited for their son, grandson, nephew, and the like. I even had a conversation with his mother a few days before the wedding when she told me all the reasons why she felt I wasn't good enough. Then on the night of the wedding rehearsal his relatives made it clear to me just how unhappy they were with me. Even the pastor who did our premarital counseling indicated there could be problems if we happened to not evolve together. Determined to make our relationship work we forged on.

The relationship with my father continued to be strained during our engagement. Things had gotten so bad that I hadn't spoken to him for months leading up to the wedding. About a week prior to the big day, I decided to give him a call. He had missed so much of my life and in spite of the ways we were divided, I loved him and didn't want him to miss any more of it. I told him I wanted him to walk me down the aisle with my mother. My mother, I felt deserved this role, yet I couldn't help but long for him to share the stage with her. This day was one of the most important days in my life. I felt it signified that in spite of where I came from, what I had done, who I was once, that I too was worthy of receiving pure, unadulterated love.

My $18,000 annual income as an Americorps worker, and the little means both our families had to contribute to our wedding, forced Curtis to borrow against his retirement to pay for most of the wedding along with an all-inclusive honeymoon in Jamaica. My mother bought my dress and my uncle Haba contributed $500 towards my flowers. I bought Curtis a Movado watch as a gift which, at a whopping $400, was a stretch for my measly salary.

The night of my bachelorette party was full of debauchery thanks to my sister Dayo–from having a party bus transport us to nightclubs, to the check box shirt my sister got me where I had to do scandalous things like have a man give me his underwear (thank you Jahir). Needless to say, I woke up the next day with a hangover from hell and vowed to be done with smoking marijuana for good. The next day, between being exhausted and nauseous and all the things that went wrong, like my hair being nothing like I wanted, my bridesmaid Olivia missing in action, my brother Jimiyu's pants for ring bearing not fitting, and my jewelry being nowhere to be found, I had a major meltdown and delayed the wedding by about forty minutes. With my father's and mother's arms entwined with my own as I walked down the aisle towards Curtis, none of that mattered. I was officially entering into a new domain that felt perfect.

When we returned from Jamaica, it really sunk in that since Curtis worked second shift and I worked hours aligned more with a first shift schedule, we would rarely ever see each other. I didn't like the idea of seeing my husband so little, but I knew there wasn't much I could do about it except wait and be grateful for what was. He tried to get hired onto the first shift and then the third shift, but turnover for these shifts rarely happened. Miraculously, a month after we were married a third shift position opened up.

When we first got married, I still had my studio apartment and Curtis was in the process of buying us a house. A month later we moved in. As I walked through this home that was built in the mid-1800s, and was painted Barney purple with turquoise trim, with a claw foot tub, hardwood floors, built-in shelves, and a high arched ceiling, it was hard to believe it was mine. That he was mine. And this was my life.

All was going well except when it came to sex. Up until the wedding, we engaged in sex quite frequently, and honestly couldn't get enough of each other. Since we had gotten married, outside of our honeymoon, I had nearly lost my sex drive. And when I would attempt to have sex it often ended in me having a flashback about my rape. For a year this went on, until one day that feeling just subsided. In spite of this, I never initiated sex, we rarely ever made out, and kissing wasn't something I particularly enjoyed. This never stopped Curtis from initiating. And he remained patient with me as I worked to find my way.

When I found out I was pregnant in September 2004 I was devastated. Not because I didn't want children, in fact, I always envisioned having two children—a boy and a girl—and would have had twins if I could have it my way. But I thought I would have more time. The ideal age to begin motherhood was closer to thirty, not twenty-five, in my mind. I kept thinking that I was just starting my life, learning what it felt like to be settled, starting to find joy for myself, and now I would have another human to look after. I didn't want to be responsible for someone else. I was just starting to figure out what it meant for me to be responsible for myself, from a place of wholeness. I had been on birth control, but I often found myself forgetting to take it, so I would double and triple up in those moments thinking that would do the trick to prevent me from getting pregnant. After my clockwork period didn't come, and my doctor's office called me with the results while I was at work, I was in shock. What should have been a joyous moment for me wasn't at all. I called Curtis immediately to share the news and that I was coming home to process. He said he would meet me, and for hours after he arrived I cried on and off as he consoled me on the couch. We watched movies and ate microwave popcorn.

One of the biggest things that initially worried me about being pregnant was that Curtis was still working third shift. I pondered how the baby and I would do in the middle of the night without him. And again, magically, a month later a first shift position opened up.

I also worried about finishing college since I still had about a year to go before I got my bachelor's degree. I had worked so hard to get here and I didn't want to throw away my dream of being college-educated simply because I was going to be a mother. Determined to complete my degree, I decided I wouldn't focus too much on this and felt confident I would get to the finish line.

For the months that followed, and the more than eighty pounds of weight I gained, we were happy. I worked up until the day I went into labor. It was thirty-six hours before I actually brought our precious daughter into the world through an emergency C-section. When I finally awoke from the anesthesia, I was shocked to see our baby girl was a mere seven pounds six ounces, considering I had gained so much weight that I was waddling by my third trimester. Curtis and I would laugh every time I went to the doctor and they would tell me how much more weight existed on my five feet four inch frame versus his six foot two inch frame. Let me confess that it was me who would make a joke about this, and Curtis would simply follow suit to be kind. He would always express how much he loved me and ask me not to worry about my weight. Not only did his words represent how much he loved me in spite of how big I had gotten, but so did his actions. He catered to me in every way, even if that meant going to get a blueberry pie close to midnight to fulfill my cravings. On one particular day, when my cravings had gotten out of control, he brought a dozen of Krispy Kremes to my job. After wolfing down five in front of him in a matter of minutes, he gently took the box from me, and said, *"Babe, I think you've had enough."* I complied because I knew his actions always came from a place of love.

After those early days of being dismayed by my pregnancy I found myself celebrating this milestone for Curtis and myself. I read everything I could about pregnancy, took classes, and was excited to design our daughter's room. We even purchased her first book, which Curtis picked, *On the Day You Were Born* by Debra Frasier, during my third trimester. I read it to her while she was in my womb, with one hand placed over my belly, more times than I can quantify. These readings would take place in a rocking chair that would become my favorite dwelling place with our daughter.

During my pregnancy I banked all my PTO which equated to thirteen weeks of paid time off so that I could be home with my daughter. I was also able to make arrangements to work second shift hours once I returned, except for two days a month when I'd have to teach classes for the not-for-profit housing organization I worked for. That meant we only had to put our daughter in daycare two full days a month. Curtis' mom had retired in the midst of our pregnancy so she was more than willing to help out however and whenever we needed her.

By my six-week check-up, mainly as a result of my choice to breastfeed, I had lost sixty pounds of the weight I had gained during pregnancy. Neither my eating nor exercise routine had changed much, so I knew it had to be the nursing.

I also graduated with my bachelor's degree around that time. Part of celebrating the completion of my degree was for me to travel out of the country for the very first time. My friend Stella had dreamed of going to Prague and Venice for as long as she could remember. Outside of the adventure that came along with exploring new places, she had her heart set on *Murano* beads for jewelry making. She had been banking airline miles for years and had enough for us both to fly there. All I had to do was have money for lodging, activities, and food. Although I was going to be gone for ten days, Curtis fully supported the trip, and assured me that between him and his mom, they would have everything covered. For months leading up to our trip, I froze enough breastmilk so our daughter's nursing schedule wouldn't be interrupted. I also took my pump with me to help my body stay in the rhythm of nursing.

Being in Venice and Prague were dreams come true. I was determined to do as much as I could while I was there which meant I was often on my own. Stella was in bed much of the time because of back pain. I felt badly that she wasn't in a position to experience the fullness of both countries. On the days she didn't feel up to exploring, I made sure she didn't need anything before I left, and would return in time to at least have the majority of our meals together.

When the trip was over, I knew I would never be the same. I wanted to see as much of the world as possible and although our combined income didn't amount to much after monthly expenses, I never even considered that Curtis and I wouldn't be able to have a life full of worldly adventures.

I'll never forget the way my daughter acted when I arrived home. For the first few minutes she not only wouldn't come to me, but she refused to look in my direction. It was amusing, but it also hurt me deeply at the time. Even at six-months-old, her feelings were crystal clear. She wanted me to know that she wasn't happy with me. I'd like to say that would be the first time she would feel intense emotions as a result of the way I chose to live in the midst of motherhood–from graduate school, to trips Curtis and I took without her, to traveling for work. I missed things that although I knew I couldn't have back, I wished I could at times. I was there a lot. I scheduled every doctor's appointment and was also present for them all. I attended every recital. I coordinated and attended every conference. We did all kinds of family activities together, from traveling to the beach, to the park, and to museums. But I still missed things and it haunted me at times. Yet I knew that was the price I had to pay to be fully who I was and what I was longing to become.

One day when she was three I was watching her dance. There was a freedom she embodied that was intriguing. And I knew at that moment that the kind of love I had for her not only had the power to hurt me, but would hurt me, because when you love someone so profoundly you will be hurt by them. That's inevitable.

Around that same time, I decided to venture into the world of consulting and entrepreneurship, which I knew absolutely nothing about. I didn't know anyone who was an entrepreneur, yet, when I would interface with consultants, I could see myself as one. So I started researching everything I could about the field. One of the most significant things I discovered was that there were state-wide and national consulting pools I could get vetted into. Even though I had never consulted a day in my life, I figured I would go for it. Even if I was vetted for the pools, this didn't guarantee work, but the possibility alone that someone would discover me and potentially want to work with me was enough. So I applied, and it paid off. Within a matter of weeks, I had my first consulting gig in Portland,

Oregon. Although this was an after-hours conference session, which meant there was no guarantee that people would actually show up, getting paid more money than I had ever earned in my life was well worth the trip.

After that first project, I was sold on becoming a consultant and a year later I was leaving my salaried job with good benefits, including two weeks vacation, for something that couldn't promise me any of that. Not only couldn't consulting promise me any of that, there were no guarantees for the Thurgood Marshall graduate school funding I had been placed on a waitlist for, either. Nor the grant funds I applied for to co-found the Kalamazoo Children's Defense Fund (CDF) Freedom Schools program set to hopefully begin that summer. What I did have was $9,000 saved from the consulting work that I had been doing during my vacation time, a few consulting pools, and my network. But, more than anything I had faith.

Just three days before my last day of work, everything fell into place. Full funding for CDF Freedom Schools, a Thurgood Marshall Fellowship that would pay for all my graduate school along with funds to work as an office assistant, and a consulting project that would carry me for the first few months were all lined up. If there was a time I ever questioned being cared for by Source/Universe/God/Creator, that was no longer the case. What I didn't know, however, was that I was actually co-creating this magic. I wouldn't begin to discover my power fully, however, until about ten years later when I read *E Squared* by Pam Grout.

By the time I was officially in the Thurgood Marshall Fellowship, I had taken a couple courses in counseling psychology. When I initially got the urge to go back to school, after vowing never to engage in formal education again, I couldn't shake this pull to understand what drives humans to do what they do. This urge felt outside of myself, but I also believed that the desire to explore this had something to do with my own lived experience of pain. At the time I didn't have the language to describe what I endured as a child as trauma. I also wasn't aware that I had some serious healing to do. These truths were out of my reach. The truth I did know, however, was that I was being drawn to help people work through mental and emotional blocks, therefore I was going to move in that direction.

For thirty-eight years I had lived with trauma and not even a graduate degree in clinical mental health was enough to help me see that I, too, needed intense trauma recovery work. I had run a CDF Freedom Schools program, a consulting company, and founded Be Well Beautiful Woman. I was a mother and wife and a community leader. My childhood was in the past and I was clearly moving forward, until one day it all came crashing down. Once I would start the healing journey I would discover a part of myself that was so deeply hidden that when it came to the surface it nearly shattered my world and everything in it.

But years before that, during the time of launching Kalamazoo CDF Freedom Schools, I met a man named Jomo whom I immediately felt drawn to. I knew he felt it too by the way he went out of his way to interact with me. I had been married for five years and he had been seriously dating a woman he had known since high school. I couldn't believe he had lived in Kalamazoo before he transitioned to Miami and our paths had never crossed. Jomo had even gone to the same church as Curtis and I.

That January after we first met, we spent the majority of our time with each other during training at *Alex Haley Farm*. We walked next to each other during transitions between buildings, sat at the same table during movies and meals, and we found all kinds of reasons to be in each other's presence. Like the time he asked if he could come to my room during chapel. He sat at the desk as I lay on the bed studying Gestalt's Chair Therapy Technique for graduate school. Subtle flirting was always present but more than anything it was the potent energy that existed between us. There was an ease about us, but neither one of us crossed an overt line, although it became close through the many Facebook messages and texts we exchanged starting immediately after we left training.

I couldn't lie to myself, I wanted him, and often spoke, and sometimes cried, with my mom about it. This is when crystal clear feelings started coming to the surface that I wasn't happy, not just in my marriage, but within myself–although that part I had yet to realize. Regardless of what I felt, or what he felt, we maintained pretty firm unspoken boundaries. Until he came into town one weekend for work.

I told Curtis that he and I were going to meet for dinner and drinks.

As any night, Curtis trusted me and that I'd be home at a decent hour. Jomo and I went to Zazios for small plates and live music and then moved on to Burdicks for drinks. Before I realized it, it was after 11:30 p.m. I figured I'd stay just a little bit longer and that turned into shutting down Burdicks and we were getting into my car, wasted. It turned into a full make-out session for hours. The last time I texted Curtis was at 11:30 p.m. I told him not to wait up and I'd be home soon. We didn't have sex that night, but came close. When I finally stopped us, and insisted I take him back to his hotel, it was nearly 5 a.m. I panicked. I had no idea what I was going to tell Curtis.

After Jomo was in the hotel, I just sat there reflecting on what I had just done. I felt nauseous. I took some deep breaths and told myself that everything was going to be okay. I then scripted a story about leaving Burdick's drunk around 1 a.m. and being so inebriated that I sat in my car to try to sober up and had passed out instead. I contemplated all the questions Curtis might ask me. Like why Jomo didn't walk me to the car. I'd say that he attempted to but I told him over and over again that I was fine to drive, but I didn't realize I actually wasn't okay until I walked out to my car. If he asked why I didn't call him at the time, I'd say I intended to sit for a few minutes to get my grounding before heading home, that more than anything I felt sick, versus drunk, and that if I could just rest a little I thought I'd be fine making it home. If he asked me if there was flirting, I would repeat that he was simply my homeboy, updates on his now wife and their children, our work with CDF Freedom Schools, and the like.

Stating once again that it was nothing but a platonic friendship. I felt prepared for all of it, so I got into my car, and headed home, consciously breathing every second of the way.

It took a lot of work to get out of that situation, but days later, as skeptical as I knew Curtis was, we settled back into our lives, and I began distancing myself more and more from Jomo. From that day forward, I became finely tuned in to the attraction I felt to other men, and the attraction they felt for me. In those moments, I would resist the temptation to explore, even a little, in order to diligently work to honor my relationship with Curtis, and what we had built. And for years that worked. I dodged this energy in all kinds of ways. Diverting my energy towards their wives and partners, avoiding them altogether, being aloof and self-absorbed, anything that would take my energy away from getting pulled into something I knew had the power to hurt Curtis. And then I met Kali.

I wasn't attracted to Kali when I first met her–at all. Well, I was attracted to her energy, but that was it. And in fact my attraction to women only manifested itself when Curtis and I would go on vacation and I'd be drawn to a waitress, for example. I would be blatant about my attraction to women and had even explored the possibility of having a threesome with a woman, which Curtis always seemed open to, but never initiated. I simply didn't have the courage to actually do anything except talk in secret about it.

My attraction to females was always present. In fact, my first memory of kissing a girl was when I was five, and although I hadn't kissed a girl since I was in fifth grade, my attraction to them never subsided–from women I worked with, to friends of mine. At times, I felt many of them were attracted to me too, but no one ever had the courage to do a damn thing about it.

So from fifth grade until Curtis, I had only been with males.

Kali had a way with people that seemed to attract them to her magnetically. She had this uncanny ability of contorting herself into what you wanted her to be. And it wasn't that she wasn't these things, but she would illuminate parts of herself and quiet other parts of herself–depending on who she was around–in order to make a connection. The first time we spoke I was attracted to her voice instantly, and to a certain lightness about her. She was confident, bold. I had always been attracted to this quality in people. It was endearing, in general, but especially for girls and women because of the messages we absorb, making us feel at times that we have to appear less powerful in order to be accepted.

When we first connected I had a feeling she was going to be someone that could help elevate me and my work, and a relationship was forged. During our first official business meeting, I could tell by the way she looked at me that she was attracted to me. I thought, *"Oh shit! What am I going to do to quiet this so we can have a productive business relationship?"* In that instant I made clear through my energy that I wasn't open to that kind of attraction and that seemed to do the trick.

By the end of the first week, I discovered a lot about Kali. The relationship she had with her two brothers was strained, which caused her emotional distress because it made building a relationship with her niece and nephew feel impossible. I discovered how much she adored her parents but that she still often felt like the black sheep of the family because of her sexuality, gender expression, and other more liberal beliefs she held in opposition to her family, rooted in a homogeneous farming community close to Northern Michigan. I learned that she had been married for about a year and took great pride in being Kaitlyn's wife.

Although people told me things all the time, I was surprised that Kali was so adamant about telling me so much, so soon. At the end of each story, she would say, *"This is just who I am."* I felt this level of openness was odd because we barely knew each other, and especially because I was such a private person. People told me all kinds of things about their lives, and would typically blurt out midpoint or at the end, *"I can't believe I'm telling you this,"* or, *"I've never told anyone this before,"* or, *"This is so bizarre but I feel comfortable telling you this."* I felt this was a privilege. These moments felt sacred to me. The fact that people knew they could trust me was a gift that I never wanted to take for granted. And Kali was simply doing what others had done. So why did it feel so off?

That summer Curtis and I went to Antigua to celebrate our fifteenth wedding anniversary, and a month later, in August, we were in Kenya having the time of our lives on vacation as a family. Just weeks later, I found Kali increasingly filling my thoughts. By the middle of September, I knew I wanted her–bad. We had become so in sync that we'd wake up at the same time in the wee hours of the morning–between 2 a.m. and 4 a.m.–and simply start texting each other. I started finding excuses to see her and pick her brain about something.

And then one night after we came back from a business trip, Curtis, Kali, Kaitlyn, and I ended up on my patio drinking a huge bottle of red wine Kali had brought over from Costco. Curtis turned in early which left me on the loveseat alone and Kali and Kaitlynn sitting across from me in individual chairs. A couple hours later, Kali stood up out of her chair and asked if she could sit next to me. Although this made me uncomfortable, I was turned on by her boldness. I turned towards Kaitlyn and she seemed to be in her own world. Kali sat next to me and nearly instantly started rubbing my back and then my leg, insisting I was cold and she was going to warm me up. I attempted to get her to stop, honestly concerned about Kaitlyn more than anything since I was aroused by Kali's tenacity, and would have preferred her not to stop. Kali continued. They seemed to be in two separate worlds. Kali trying to get into mine, and Kaitlyn simply oblivious to anything other than herself at the moment.

The two weeks that followed were awkward and then Kali told me she might start working on another project which would mean I'd have to find another thought partner. The thought of losing Kali jolted me. I acted unphased when Kali broke down into tears, telling me how hard this was for her. I sent her on her way stoically, but I couldn't seem to shake it. All day the thought of her leaving haunted me, and that night, on my way home, I decided to stop at Crow's Nest, a spot we frequented and one of the first places our attraction was palpable. As I sat there eating tomato soup and a garden salad, I got the urge to text her. More than six hours later, it was done. I revealed to her subtly how I felt, and I believed that she felt the same way. Our affair had begun.

We communicated with each other nonstop that entire weekend. Through the 60th birthday celebration we had for my mom at The Union, sports games, drinking with friends, television with family–nothing interfered with our communication. And then when we saw each other that Monday we embraced for a long time before we just stared at each other in awe, not really knowing what to say, but not really needing to.

By week's end, we had a candid conversation about the nature of the affair. I articulated that I had no desire to leave Curtis, and she proclaimed the same thing about Kaitlyn. Uninformed about navigating an affair, I convinced myself that I could live in two worlds. One where I was "happily" married to a man, and another where I slept with a woman.

It took me a month before I held her hand, and another two weeks before we kissed. And that solidified it for me. I had gone from not liking kissing, to having my breath damn near taken away by a kiss. Now I knew what fireworks felt like. And I was determined to have it. All of it.

A couple weeks later, when we were scheduled to go to LA for business, we went all the way. After eating eggs benedict and enjoying a couple mimosas and making out on the elevator, we barely made it to our room. As soon as we got inside, we took each other's clothes off as as quickly as possible. Kali made it seem like it was going to be the most mind-blowing experience I had ever had, but her nervousness got the best of her, which left me feeling lackluster about the whole thing. Plus my period started so that put a damper on our plans.

After we returned from the trip, she made up for it. While sitting at my dining room table, I experienced the deepest orgasm I had ever felt. From there I was hooked. We fucked in church parking lots. Across from Gonzo's downtown. In the Days Inn parking lot. In the Meijer parking lot. Across from a park. At share ride lots. Everywhere. And we became reckless.

It didn't matter what we had going on, we would find a way to see each other. Even on Thanksgiving, I left at night to console her after she had gotten into a fight with her in-laws, and ultimately Kaitlyn. I didn't like the thought of her being upset and I made it my mission to shield her from hurting to the best of my ability, even if that meant I was hurting myself and those around me in the process.

Just seven weeks from the time the affair started, Curtis found out. He knew something was gravely off. It came to him in dreams. He woke up in the middle of the night and found text messages from Kali at 3 a.m. He felt my energy shifting as I started falling in love with

Kali and out of love with him. He asked me about it on a few occasions but I always lied. When Kali and I returned from a business trip in New York, he went through my emails and found several she had written confessing her love. He woke me up around 2 a.m. to ask me about it, and then stormed out of the house in tears when I finally admitted what he already knew.

When he returned a couple hours later I was in the living room waiting on him. I told him everything. Not just about Kali, but about Jomo, too. Although I knew these truths would break us, I also knew I couldn't carry them anymore.

Chapter 12
Heartbreak & Healing

By the first week in January, roughly a month after Curtis found out about the affair, I moved into Jonbenet's small vacant house tucked away behind the fairgrounds. I had visited this house on several occasions before but today the neighborhood looked different. The small houses appeared to be even smaller with the white fluffy snow piled on top of the roofs. They also looked duller with the brown snowy slush covering the streets, coupled with their pale yellow, green, and dusty white paint that draped the frames. The closer we got to the house, the tinier I felt. My surroundings seemed to cave in on me. I breathed deeply as we approached the driveway. When we were finally parked, I looked up at the white home with faded blue trim, surrounded by a silver chain-link fence, and a porch that appeared to be separating from the home, and thought to myself, *this is my new normal.*

Curtis helped me unpack our cars with the few belongings I had taken to start my new life.

With only my artwork in tow, along with a few bags of clothes, shoes, my laptop, and the like, I entered this small space that seemed to be straight out of an old movie. Looking at the white walls, shaggy brown carpet, and beige color palette that surrounded me I felt nothing. I had gone from a home filled with vibrant colors where I had participated in every aspect of the design to a place that felt as if it had no pulse.

The house consisted of a tiny kitchen with a pub style table and two chairs facing the wall closest to the bedroom where my daughter would sleep when she came home every other week. The bathroom was so condensed that with the toilet and small corner shower, there was only standing room for a single person. I would sleep in the living room which contained a Queen bed, small brown leather sectional, a tan plywood desk, and 52" tv and stand. This had all been left behind by my brother, and I was welcome to use it. The only thing I didn't have access to was the locked bedroom where his belongings were stored. This gave me roughly four hundred square feet to enjoy.

I hadn't lived in a space this small since before I was married. I loved my studio apartment that was adjacent to a home in a beautiful neighborhood off West Main street. It was a mini version of the home I built with Curtis and our daughter. This home wasn't mine though, and although my artwork would make it feel more like mine, I couldn't bring myself to put it on the walls. It wasn't until months later, when my friend Margaret was visiting and she inquired why I hadn't put my Angela Davis piece up, that I finally got the gumption to hang my art.

That first night as I lay in bed completely alone, absorbing unfamiliar sounds, smells, and sights, I felt the magnitude of this new world I had stepped into. I desperately wanted to disappear, for it all to go away, but I knew that wasn't possible. Instead, I allowed the tears to flow, placed my hands over my chest, and breathed deeply until I drifted off to sleep.

During the first few months in my new place, there were countless adjustments I had to make, but the biggest was getting used to the amount of time I spent alone. Curtis and I agreed on joint custody so that meant I would only be with our daughter every other week. On weeks I wasn't with her, I assumed my time would be filled with Kali considering we had fallen head over heels in love. We saw each other quite a bit in the beginning, but as time progressed, our fighting increased which caused our relationship to become increasingly strained. The more I sought answers about the nature of her relationship with Kaitlyn, the more we fought. The more we fought, the more time and space separated us.

Kali and Kaitlyn continued to live together after the separation. Kali would step away to talk to her when she called and when we were together. When I needed Kali most–during times of intense emotional distress–she was nowhere to be found and would make me feel bad for needing her support. We fought, one of us would leave, and then we would come back together, after hours, and sometimes days, of having no contact.

I had traded a loving marriage for what started to feel like an unrequited love. Although I knew happiness ebbed and flowed for years in my marriage, I thought I was ultimately where I was supposed to be. Curtis was always kind, loving, and supportive. We had built this beautiful life together for fifteen years and in a matter of months I decided to throw it all away. Even if Curtis and I could find our way back to each other, I was at a minimum bi-sexual, and I had no desire to close off that part of myself. Plus, I didn't know if I could love him again. I knew I would always love him, but I had fallen out of love with him in the process of falling in love with Kali.

As I thought more and more about my life in its present state, I trampled on opportunities that allowed me to understand the power I had to change. I started to discover that life wasn't happening to me, it was happening for me. And it was ultimately up to me to decide how I was going to live my one precious life, as Mary Oliver so famously said.

I had first been introduced to the concept of co-creation a couple years before my separation when I read Pam Grout's, *E Squared*. Then I landed on Reiki–a spiritual energy practice involving light touch over the major organ centers which helped me realize that I could ignite my body's natural ability to heal itself. I felt so aligned with the impacts of Reiki, that I adopted a consistent daily practice and started feeling all kinds of positive effects. It gave me increased energy, greater clarity, helped me release negative emotions, and I felt more resilient.

Not long after, I completed a trauma-informed yoga certification which exponentially increased my understanding of trauma and its impact on the whole body. I then said yes to attending a healing group centering Gabrielle Bernstein's *May Cause Miracles*. I was completely oblivious to the way those six weeks were going to change my life. Through that exploration, I realized that joy and peace was mine for the taking–fully and completely–and that through my thoughts I could channel these emotions any time I chose.

There were countless moments like this that followed. They often seemingly came from nowhere; but as the *Course in Miracles* says, what we are seeking is seeking us, so these moments weren't random. They were divine. All of it was divine.

It was in those moments that I started to face myself. It was also in those moments that I was able to accept things as they were. It gave me the freedom to not only deal with what came from my continued choice to be with Kali, but anything else that life threw at me. It didn't mean that I wasn't affected, but I could bounce back more easily, sometimes in a matter of seconds. I would move my attention to more loving thoughts which allowed me to choose happiness regardless of what was surfacing in my life.

It became clear that when I consistently cultivated these practices, I felt better. The more I centered wellness, the more I became well. And the more I became well, the more I felt joy, peace, creativity, and an overall zest for life. Abundance, I perceived, flowed from this place, flowed from me. As I drew within, I drew closer to the Source/Universe/God/Creator, and from there, with intention, I could curate whatever I desired for my life.

In May, after discovering Kaitlynn had spent the weekend with Kali, from photos that miraculously showed up in my Facebook feed despite the fact that we weren't friends nor had any overlapping contacts, I was devastated. The weekend centered around the wedding of Kali's best friend, Hailey. Kali was a bridesmaid. We fought the entire weekend which gave her room to be mostly unavailable. I knew at that moment I should be done with her. Everything in me was screaming "leave" except, of course, my heart, so I stayed. I couldn't bear the thought of not having her in my life.

Later that day, I cried in the kitchen I had just renovated with Curtis a year prior, and he consoled me as I expressed how stupid I was for allowing myself to be in this situation that had caused us all immense pain. I had always known that Curtis loved me, but this was a demonstration of love that far exceeded the kind of love most of the world bears witness to. It was the kind of love that bell hooks described in *All About Love - the will to extend one's self for the purpose of nurturing one's own or another's spiritual growth* that he bestowed to me that day. I'll forever be grateful for that, especially because there was a part of me that didn't believe I deserved this kind of love after what I had done to destroy our family.

By June, Kali moved to Chicago to start a new job. During the move I was in Charlotte, North Carolina for the *Black Enterprise Entrepreneurs Summit*. I had gotten used to fighting a lot with Kali, but this week the fighting seemed to be more intense, especially when I would bring up coming to see her when I returned. The night before I was scheduled to go home, I discovered that Kaitlyn would be staying with Kali supposedly for a couple weeks until she moved to South Carolina for a work transfer. I couldn't believe what I was hearing. I had obliterated the parts of my life I had known the most, that were most important to me, for what I believed was a love that was worthy. This was nowhere in the vicinity.

I blocked Kali on my phone and all social media platforms. Email was the only way she could communicate with me. The first thing she wrote to me was simply, *"Not gonna let me explain?"* Email exchanges filled with her telling me about Juneteenth, to *"I'm sorry,"* to justifying her actions went on for eleven days, and on the twelfth day she sent me this:

I have been running, waking up every morning and running. I have changed my diet drastically. I only eat fruits and veggies, barely any carbs, and LOTS of chicken. I spend most of my nights working on the house, doing projects inside and out, spending time with the dogs. They love being with me all the time . . . it's so crazy how much they enjoy being in my space. There is a river in the backyard, they love watching the ducks and geese go by, gives them something to do. The squirrels and birds are savage. They wait until the last minute to run from the boys and Jude has nearly caught a few of them. My mom put in an application for a management position at a new hospital and got a call that same day. She goes in for her interview Thursday. She sent me some questions and has been using me for help and support getting her ready for the interview. It's kinda bizarre, especially because she's got fifteen years of management experience. My brothers were complete asses on Fathers Day . . . didn't get dad a card, just showed up and golfed. I paid for his golf, got him a card, and made him dinner. I swear I don't understand, especially because I am not 100% happy with him at this point in time, but I still made the day about him.

All I wanted to do since Kali and I started was be part of her world. These words somehow made me feel like I was. I longed for her exponentially more than I had since I disconnected her from my life. I wrote back:

Reading all this made me super emotional. I unblocked you so I could tell you that, but you forwarded me to voicemail so either you're busy or simply didn't want to speak to me. I don't even know if I'm ready to talk to you so I blocked you again. It's my process, so please let it be. I'm glad that things are going so well in your life. Especially after going through such hardship these last several months.

And Kali's response to me:

I am sorry it made you emotional. I just started typing, feeling like I needed to tell you some of the things in my world for the last few weeks. I'm sorry you called and it went to voicemail–I have blocked you as well. It's helped me not constantly check my phone or feel the urge to contact you, as you have cut me off and I wasn't going to sit here and wonder when it would be over. Things in my life are average, the best things I have are that I am with my dogs everyday, I sleep in my bed, and that this case is finally coming to a close soon.

I won't question your process, as I have realized that YOU in totality, how you process, as well as your decision making, I would never understand. And after you cut me off, I am starting to realize

214

that I never really will. We have been a complete fuck-all mess since December, we never really bounced back from that weekend . . . we've tried, but it never actually happened. You can blame me all you want, for you to cut me off, have your space, and the like, and I have come to terms with that. But I want you to think about all the decisions you made that hurt me, that you didn't include me on, that you disregarded my feelings, and opinions on . . . I never once cut you off like this. Today, I realized how you've handled this hurt, me making a decision that I did not include you on, is ok, because we are different people. Through all of this, you learned one major thing about me. Space isn't good for me, it never did me, nor us, any justice and yet you continue to use it.

That was the beginning of allowing Kali to make me believe I was somehow at fault for her actions. There would be countless times during the relationship when she would tell me I was being difficult, or asking for too much, or that my tactics, like space, when she would harm me, was the catalyst for her wrongdoing. *It was my fault that so much distance existed between us. If only I didn't ask so much of her then things would be different.*

Kali making decisions that kept me on the outskirts of her life became a recurring theme in our relationship. Along with the justification to not include me in decisions and also not tell me about them. I would often discover these things on my own. Like when she moved back to the area from Chicago and was living in a modular home on Kaitlynn's parents' land. Or when she moved into her new house, that Kaitlynn had moved in as well.

On top of lies I caught her in, and things she simply omitted to tell me, we fought about the lack of time she made available to spend with me. I continued to claw for space in her life, and she remained steadfast about keeping me out of it.

Space felt like the only safeguard I had against Kali. I didn't know what to do with the immense division that kept coming to the surface of our relationship. Ultimately I didn't know how to make her love me the way I wanted to be loved, the way I knew I was worthy of being loved. I had gone from the closest thing one can get to altruistic love with Curtis to a love that was equivalent to a war zone.

Although our fighting continued for a while following that email, a few days later we were fucking in downtown Chicago parked at a meter in the middle of the day. When we were done, I cried, and I told her I felt like the other woman. Kali convinced me that I was the only woman and in time I would see this. For the four months that followed, I drove to Chicago during the weeks I I didn't have my daughter to meet up at restaurants, bars, my friend Stacia's, and hotel rooms as I waited for Kaitlynn to take this job in South Carolina that Kali kept telling me was being held up. And then one day, after finding texts we exchanged about renovating the house, marriage, including pictures of rings and all, Kaitlyn packed up her things and left. I was there the next day. We fought so badly that first day that Kali asked me to leave and I landed at my friend Stacia's. I cried for hours that night in bed. The next day I was back with Kali.

Although Kali was now living alone and I was spending a good deal of my time with her, she continued to tenaciously keep her life separate from mine. We weren't connected on social media. She and Kaitlynn maintained the same friends. When Kali would host something at her house, Kaitlynn was always present. And of course I was never invited. Kaitlynn's presence, and my absence weren't the only issues–it was that Kali would lie about Kaitlynn attending.

Lying was the norm with Kali. She lied about buying the house in Chicago on her own. Kaitlynn had actually purchased the house with Kali which I discovered when Kali gave me access to her email password to check her flight itinerary. She lied about trips she'd claim she was going on solo with her friends, all to find out that Kaitlynn was also in attendance. She even lied about getting a divorce which I uncovered eight months later. This one particular day I felt the urge to Google her and found Kaitlynn's bio naming them still married and living happily together with their four dogs and two cats. Kali was so calculated that the day of the supposed divorce she fought with me because she indicated I hadn't properly supported her.

Although we went out in public often, gala's and all, we mainly ran into people I knew, and on the rare occasion we'd see someone Kali knew, she never introduced me. To anyone who happened to see us out, our energy and the way we physically interacted with each other, not to mention the fighting, made it clear we were together, and yet we lived in completely unconnected worlds with none of our social circles overlapping.

I was the other woman–had always been the other woman. Regardless of what Kali claimed about Kaitlynn, her actions spoke volumes about where I stood in relation to them. Although I hated it, and it hurt me to my core to be on the sidelines of her life, I knew there was nothing that I could do to change that.

Each time I'd leave, it became easier for me to stay away for longer periods of time. Twelve days of not seeing each other the first time I cut her off, turned to six months of not seeing each other during the last time we broke up. It wasn't emotionally easy for me however. Kali's energy constantly tugged on me. It took immense strength for me to resist the urge to contact her. And outside of my daughter, she remained my most constant thought. Every song I heard reminded me of her, and no matter where I went or what I did, "she" seemed to be there. There were waitresses named Kali, someone would say something just like she would, movie scenes were reminiscent of us, and the list goes on. Everything seemed to be about her. At times it felt like I couldn't escape.

As I traversed through our relationship, the focus on my wellness increased through training, books, and being in community with those who were also on the path to enlightenment. Joy and peace became my number one priority, and my life increasingly started to change as a result. Abundance was showing up in every area of my life except with Kali. I started to express this to her, and mentioned that if things didn't change I would ultimately leave. I was determined to live well, even if that meant being without her.

The last time I left, although I had proclaimed it thousands of times before, I believed it was for good. I hadn't felt rage towards Kali in a few years, but when she told me that Kaitlynn moved back in with her temporarily so she could save for a house, without even discussing it with me, I snapped. I told her she was the worst human on the planet, along with a few other things, and blocked her again.

A couple months later Kali reached out to me twice-once through text and once through email. *"You were on my mind tonight."* was all she said, all within a matter of minutes. I didn't respond, and then a couple months later, it was like her spirit entered mine while I was writing, and for the first time in months I really missed her. I reached out through text only to realize she blocked me; I then sent her an email.

Hi! It's been a minute :). Although there is space and time between us I want you to know there isn't a day that goes by when I don't think about you. You still remain my most constant thought. I often send love and light your way-my hope is you can feel it although I'm not present. These last few days I've thought about how we started-all the details and the possibility of what could be. I'm appreciating remembering us in this way. I hope you're healthy and happy. I think you know I will always love you-no matter what.

That evening she sent me a text message asking me what prompted my email and we were right back at it.

For more than five years this pattern of fighting and retreating ensued. There would be periods of honeymoon, but that would last for no more than three weeks before we were right back to not speaking to each other, seeing each other, or simply fighting. When it was good, it was good, but mostly it was bad, mired with deep pain and a separation that seemed to be perfectly normal for Kali, but was killing me.

The heart wants what it wants. I knew who Kali was before I dove into the relationship and yet I felt the love she had for me would shield me from her harm. Lying and secrets had been part of her survival since she was a child due to her own trauma, but I somehow believed she wouldn't lie to me. As in the words of Don Miguel Ruiz in *The Four Agreements*, "Wherever you go you will find people lying to you, and as your awareness grows, you will notice that you also lie to yourself. Do not expect people to tell you the truth because they also lie to themselves. You have to trust yourself and choose to believe or not to believe what someone says to you." When there is a pattern of lying, we can be rest assured that we will also be lied to. If we don't believe that, or chose not to see it, then we are also lying to ourselves.

We tell ourselves that we're different. We believe somehow that we are special, and our specialness will shield us from the very wrongdoing we see the ones we love bestowing upon others. We believe that people will change, not because we necessarily have evidence of this, but simply because we want them to change. We see what someone could be versus who they really are. As Maya

Angelou said, "When people show you who they are, believe them the first time." This doesn't mean that people can't change, or won't change, but it does mean this is who they are right now. If you accept the truths of who someone is at the present moment, then you're also accepting what comes along with that truth.

My healing journey led me to the moment when I finally had enough love within myself to break away for good. Breaking away from unrequited love is massive work. And when that love is unlike any kind of love you've ever experienced, it's easy to latch onto. It becomes an addiction. What I've come to realize is my deep attraction to Kali was, in part, a manifestation of my trauma. My past traumatic experiences gave me a distorted perception of what it meant to love and be loved, and I was willing to endure all kinds of things I thought I never would in its name.

The truth is, I would have never stayed with Kali for more than five years had I really loved myself. After the first time I became aware of her deception, I would have left. But that simply wasn't in the divine plan. I needed those five years to do deep healing work so I could see myself more clearly. And that space between us that kept widening, which started out with me leaving for twelve days, then six weeks, then four and a half months, then six months, until I could do it forever, was driven by the ongoing investment in my healing.

Although I am still very much in love with Kali, and miss her so much it hurts at times, staying would hurt much more. I finally understand and fully embrace that Kali is not good for me, and that I, as much as Kali, have been responsible for harm in our relationship. I can't lie though, I wish I would have listened when my brother Jimiyu told me, five months into the relationship, to be done with her–along with the countless times that my friends and family told me the same thing. I loved her too much to be done. I hoped things would change. I was fixated on what could be versus what had been staring me in the face all along.

I had allowed myself to get roped into a narcissistic, abusive relationship. Facing that the culmination of my complex childhood trauma, more than twenty-five years earlier, ended in me being in a relationship that catapulted me to some of the darkest moments I have ever experienced, and allowed, has been hard to accept.

It's difficult to think that I, the therapist and holistic healer who had spent her entire career helping care for others and supporting them in centering their healing and liberation, was caught up in an emotionally abusive relationship. Admitting that to myself, let alone to the world, has been downright stupefying, and it's important to acknowledge that it happened. My trauma, unbeknownst to me, drove me to this.

We live in a world where we make a lot of assumptions about who the face of abuse is, and yet there are people from all walks of life that have survived trauma or are currently in abusive relationships–some of which we know. They're our next door neighbors. Our colleagues. Even our family and friends. And sometimes they are people just like me, who are working to change the very communities they live in. We show up with smiles in public, but are often suffering in silence.

Abuse can happen to any of us, especially when we are carrying past abuse. This is why acknowledging the trauma we have endured is so critical, along with understanding how that very trauma is manifesting in our lives. We can't heal the things we refuse to face. And although facing these things will be the most difficult task we ever take on, it will be the most rewarding. Once the pain subsides, then the light can come in and we can discover our true nature. We are meant to live joyfully, peacefully, and abundantly in every way but we can't get there without facing the darkness that trauma creates. As the saying goes, although we didn't ask to be harmed, if we choose to not heal then we are technically choosing our own suffering. So choose wisely, because no matter who you are, and what you've been through you deserve love, joy, peace, financial wealth, pleasure, and more.

I often say that healing and liberation are the great equalizers because no matter what we've been through, or where we've come from, as we center wellbeing, we regain Source-given power, which becomes the guide for co-creating with purpose. Everything in our life is a manifestation of what we've brought into it—whether we are conscious of this or not. Instead of passively co-creating, we can do so with loving intention in order to manifest the life we want, the life we are all worthy of.

The core practices that have, and will continue to support me in healing from complex childhood trauma, have included yoga, Reiki, being in nature, journaling, and more. Other practices that are not just good for trauma survivors, but us all, include working through grief, the practice of forgiveness, and cultivating an abundance mindset, which I wrote about in the remaining chapters.

Chapter 13
The Role Grief Plays In Trauma

You cannot prevent the birds of sorrow from flying over your head, but you can prevent them from building nests in your hair.

-Old Chinese Proverb

One typically wouldn't think of grief in the context of trauma but any form of loss, both material and human, involves the grief cycle. Although the first model of grief, called the Kubler Ross model, consists of five stages of grief including denial, anger, bargaining, depression, and acceptance, was created to help individuals understand the process one goes through when they lose someone they love, any form of grief can be applied.

Take my gang rape for example, after it first happened I went into a deep depression that led me to attempt to take my own life. While I was in the adolescent psychiatric unit I called one of my attackers, Max, to question him. I remember distinctly asking how he could do this to me. Although of course I knew that it happened, there was a part of me in denial about it. I didn't want to believe it. While the days that followed existed mainly in confinement at the hospital, my anger festered. This precipitated many altercations with the staff. A few years later, through my reintroduction to spirituality, I was able to see my attackers' full humanity which led me to forgive them all.

You may have noticed that my process didn't include bargaining. That's because we don't necessarily go through each grief stage, nor do the stages work linearly as in this example, considering I went right into a deep depression after the assault.

The grief involved in losing my father in a freak accident after he was struck by a truck and died instantly, also didn't succinctly align with each of the grief stages.

When I first found out he died, I was in disbelief. Moments later, I had an intense bout of bargaining where I expressed to God that if only He'd allow my father to resurrect, I would be a better daughter. And then within the minutes that followed, I was angry with my dad. I wondered why he didn't park his car closer to the highway overpass. I questioned why he hadn't paid more attention when he got out of the car. I wondered why he couldn't have just waited to get off the highway to get the wet wipes out of his trunk to clean the red residue from the *Hot Cheetos* that were on my niece and nephews hands. Finally, I went into isolation for days that followed, having no contact with the world except my then husband, Curtis, and our daughter. On my first day back at work, I didn't even make it into the building. My sorrow was so potent, I had to turn around, get back in my car and then drive home to return to seclusion. A few days later, I was ready to start again.

*I don't know why they call it heartbreak. It feels like every part of my body is broken too. -**Chloe Woodward***

In terms of a relationship breakup, all the grief stages can play out along with many others. I, for one, can deeply relate to the grief of ending a relationship with a partner, along with friendships. *The 13 Stages of Grief of Every Breakup* by Perri O. Blumberg and Naydeline Mejiua featured in *Women's Health,* and developed with the support of seven clinical psychologists and social workers of varying specialities, helps explain this.

1. *Ambivalence:* This is the stage where you flounder between the desire to be with someone and question the relationship. It is typically marked by "good" and "bad" days which can fuel the cycle of desire or lack thereof.
2. *Euphoric Recall:* This stage is mired in remembering all the things you enjoyed about your ex. Beautiful moments you shared. Songs you exchanged. Wild nights. Tantalizing conversations. The list is endless. The key here is that you typically forget all of the things that caused the demise of the relationship to begin with. Intentionally acknowledging the things that caused you angst in the relationship will allow for a balanced perspective to emerge, and support you in moving forward.
3. *Making Sense of It All:* During this time one obsesses about

the breakup, sifting through every detail, trying to make sense of what happened and ultimately what one or both parties could have done differently. There is a desperate search for the why and one will sometimes go to great lengths to get it. Closure is the goal here. One can certainly try to get closure by engaging in a conversation with their ex, but know that the ex can decide not to engage in the conversation, or simply not provide the answers desired. Another option is to simply let it go, accepting what is, at least for now, as none of us really knows what the future holds. This will help you find peace.

4. *Numbness:* Sometimes one can go into a form of depression that manifests a feeling of numbness. We might equate it to a zombie-like state, hollow, unsure of what we're actually feeling. This usually occurs when we're not honoring our emotions. Actively working to get out what we feel, particularly through **somatic practices like yoga, or energy healing techniques such as Reiki,** can aid you in the grieving process by removing any blocked emotions you may be unconsciously or consciously harboring.

5. *Denial:* During this stage one works to convince oneself that the relationship isn't over. This could present itself through maintaining contact with your ex, an inability to respect their boundaries, flirtation, and more. One of the

reasons why denial becomes so pervasive is that our identities may have been so wrapped up in the ex that the thought of them not being in our lives becomes unbearable. We can counter this by writing down exactly what we want in a partner, and curating a vision for living life without your ex including things you will continue to do without them and new activities to replace the old ones.

6. *Anger:* The anger stage is mired in remembering all the things your ex did to overtly harm you, everything they did to annoy you, everything you did for them and they didn't appreciate, and the list goes on. As a result, anger, and at times downright rage, can kick in. Anger certainly should be honored. It's an emotion, like any emotion, designed to teach you something. Ultimately you just don't want to stay in it too long because of the self-harm it can do. Take space to **allow your anger to flow, through journaling, hitting a pillow, screaming at the top of your lungs, kickboxing, and more.** Ultimately, try anything that's going to get your body moving and therefore the aggression out until it is next to non-existent.

7. *Bargaining:* During this time you might renege on the things you previously said were important to you that you were unwilling to compromise on with your ex. If they don't want children for example, you might try to convince yourself that having children isn't really that important to

you, all to try to save the relationship. Being honest with yourself and the vision you have for your life and your partner is critical. Go back to the list you made of what you want in a partner and make sure you honor it, no matter how badly you want that person in your life. If you compromise on things that are deeply important to you, that will only result in resentment down the road.

8. *Sadness:* The demise of a relationship can feel equivalent to the death of a loved one. It's important to feel the immense sadness that often comes along with a breakup. And it's not just the loss of them from your life that you grieve. You also have to give up on the future you desire to have with them, be that a house, kids, marriage, or vacations. During this stage one might isolate, experience appetite loss or gain, or sleep more or less. Honoring this stage, just like the others, is critical, but if these symptoms linger, preventing you from doing things you otherwise would want to, for longer than two weeks, you should probably talk to a professional, such as a therapist.

9. *Sharing the News:* The authors call this Social Media Changes but I altered it to comprise the layers of communication we engage in relative to a breakup. Sometimes we don't want to tell other people about the breakup because not only do we have to be prepared for their questions, but it also makes it that much more real.

Having conversations with loved ones to announce the breakup isn't easy but it's a step in the right direction to move through grief. Facing the truth is one of the most freeing things we can do for ourselves. Then we can ultimately share, as we feel led, on social media and with colleagues. We get to control the narrative, like whether we want to answer questions or not and how much information we divulge.

10. *Relapse:* This stage could lead to a better relationship than before as a result of changes each of you may have made, but it could also simply be a relapse. This time could be riddled with a honeymoon period that could last for a couple weeks until the issues that caused the demise of your relationship shows back up–sometimes manifesting worse than before. Depending on the dynamics of the relationship, this could occur several times. Only you can ultimately decide what is best for you since sometimes things do work out. What I would suggest is if you and your ex do indeed decide to get back together, take inventory of exactly what you want in a partner, things that are non-negotiables, and things that you struggle with and would simply like to explore. From there, engage in several open, honest, and loving conversations to talk through each of your issues. Then decide from there whether you should take that leap to reignite your

relationship.

11. *Acceptance:* When acceptance kicks in you no longer resist the notion of not being with your ex. Inevitably, you will still think of them, but you've fully accepted that you are no longer together. During this stage, you're taking concerted strides to move on with your life. This could mean a break from dating or putting yourself out there ready to love again.

12. *Comparison Dating:* Depending on how deep the attachment was to your ex, and the things you liked about them, you could find yourself, both consciously and unconsciously comparing your new dates to them. Even when you're absolutely sure you don't want to be with your ex anymore, this comparison can be actively at play, even in subtle ways. If one isn't careful they could get stuck in that cycle for years, impeding an ability to find love, or be fully satisfied with the love that comes into their life. To break free, begin tracking the times you compare mentally, or out loud, your ex to the person you're on a date with. Then set intentions not to do this. Mantras, such as, "*I will discover the unique beauty in this person,*" or "*I am open to finding new love,*" or "*I'm searching for the good in this person,*" can help set the tone for this. You can use these before the date, to yourself when you're on the date, and any time you find yourself in comparison mode.

13. **Forward Motion:** Your heart is completely open to love again. The memory of your ex rarely seems to surface and if it does you've fully accepted that the relationship is over. You're clear, from this place, on exactly what you want and are hopefully making decisions that are aligned with that vision.

And if you're coming out of an abusive relationship in any form, the process of grief becomes that much more difficult to navigate through. When verbal, mental, financial, or physical abuse is present in a relationship, the extra support of a trauma-informed grief counselor, coach, or therapist is paramount.

Grief changes shape, but it never ends. -**Keanu Reeves**

One of the biggest fallacies people have about grief is that when we get to the stage of acceptance that we somehow never feel any angst over the loss again. When in fact the depth of the loss can precipitate lingering effects for a lifetime. The frequency of these feelings diminish with time. And as we work to heal, our association with the loss will lean towards more positive emotions allowing us to live fully in spite of the loss.

Just the thought of the loss can move us to deep sorrow. At times this can seemingly come from nowhere along with coming at quite inopportune times. The key is to allow these emotions to come to the surface so you can process them and allow yourself to make room for those higher level emotions like joy, peace, and optimism. If we hold onto low frequency emotions, like sadness, it can cause us to get stuck. This results in feeling numb or rendering us unable to function. It's our body's way of shutting down because the emotions are too much for us to hold.

Emotions are energy in motion. They are meant to recycle through, teach us something, and then be released to make continuous room for the emotions that have the power to make us feel good.

Unfortunately feelings of grief can come seemingly from nowhere and not always at the most opportune times. So let's say grief related emotions come up while you're in public and you don't feel comfortable allowing yourself to let the emotions flow, prioritize allowing space to work through your emotions later. That way you can release them as quickly as possible, allowing you the energetic freedom to move on. If instead you try to force yourself not to feel, not to think about what is causing you grief, you go on mental overdrive. This actually has the opposite effect of what you want, according to a study from the University of Texas, causing you to think about it even more.

An unwillingness to experience feelings makes it impossible for us to effectively honor grief, normalize it, and integrate it into our lives. Not to mention it has a series of harmful effects. According to research from Harvard Medical School, the stress that comes from unacknowledged emotions can lead to slow digestion, gas, bloating, vomiting, and ulcers. Unacknowledged emotions is also related to a 70% greater risk **of being diagnosed with cancer** according to the University of Rochester and a shorter lifespan on average of up to 30% according to data derived by Harvard Medical School.

*Tears are the silent language of grief.-***Voltaire**

When we can see emotional outbursts as the "body's way of releasing that pent-up emotion," according to clinical psychologist Victoria Tarratt, then we can do what is necessary to keep the process of healing going.

I'll never forget years ago getting ready to take my daughter to the bus stop for school. I felt angst as I walked through my home to get ready which quickly turned to agitation. Thoughts of my late father filled my head which I told myself I didn't have time for because I needed to focus on the task at hand. I had lost my father roughly a year prior and memories of him pervaded my thoughts. It took all the energy I had to hide what I felt from my daughter. I simply didn't want her to pick up on the emotions I was harboring and risk it having a negative impact on her day.

As I walked back home I felt somber. Once back at my house I entered my foyer, closed the door behind me, and released an enormous cry that was so powerful it brought me to my knees. I wept in the same spot for about five minutes until I had no more tears left. Relief was immediately felt, which allowed me to get on with my day with immense peace.

*Pain demands to be felt.- **The Fault in Our Stars***

I learned something really important about emotions that day. That we either feel them or they get contorted into something they were never meant to be. When we try not to feel, we actually feel worse, or it gets alchemized into behaviors that harm us and others. We either feel now, or we *really* feel later. The choice is ours.

Matthew Ratcliffe defines grief as dynamic, involving shifting relations with the deceased, the living, and the social world. It entails an emotional response which includes recognizing, responding to, and adapting to loss. He goes on to say that grief incorporates, but is not exhausted by, the task of incorporating the world that used to be and the world that is now. If individuals struggle with aligning the past with the present, then they can get mired down by the loss, and therefore frozen in time.

*You can clutch the past so tightly to your chest that it leaves your arms too full to embrace the present. -**Jan Gildwell***

When the struggle to couple the past with the present is persistent, it can result in a victim mentality. The root of a victim mentality is loss of trust that happens when people either harm us directly or indirectly by not caring for us the way we perceive they should. When someone we love leaves us behind, or we lose something that is deeply connected to our identity, let's say being fired from a job, then a victim mentality can emerge.

Another way to think about this is that when we don't move past grief, it causes us to get stuck, fueled in part, by the belief that the world has it out for us.

Take this book for example, when I first started working on it more than fifteen years ago, I wrote the story from a place of solely being a victim. The stories I penned from that place consisted of everyone who harmed me as a villain which lacked compassion for what may have led them to harm me in the first place. Through the process of healing I realized that the people who harmed me were victims, too. They were victims of their circumstances which led them to act out their pain on me. This doesn't negate the harm they did nor excuse them for their behavior, but this shift allowed me to see the humanity in every single one of my aggressors, which was one of the pathways to regaining my power. I could then write from a place of being a victim and a survivor, simply stating the facts of what I endured, its impact on me, and the ways I healed.

According to the Cambridge Dictionary, a victim is someone or something that has been **hurt, damaged,** or **killed** or has **suffered**, either because of the **actions** of someone or something **else**, or because of **illness** or **chance**. Whereas a victim mentality emerges from being a victim, and is a psychological concept referring to a mindset in which a person, or group of people, tends to recognize or consider themselves a victim of the negative actions of others. According to Psyche Central, at its core, a victim mindset is rooted in trauma, distress, and the experience of pain most of the time. When someone experiences a traumatic situation, typically at the hands of other people, one may learn they are helpless and that nothing they do in the future is going to make any difference.

So many people are wandering through the world with a victim mentality, but are totally oblivious to this fact. And because we can't change things we aren't aware of, I thought it would be helpful for us to explore indicators of a victim mentality, with the help of my friends at Science of People:

- Negative self-talk or self-pity. *"I never do anything right."*
- Pessimism about the future. *"It will never work out."*
- Fears of being taken advantage of. "Bad things have happened before, so they will inevitably happen again."
- Envious of others. "If only I had money like she does."
- Ruminates on past bad experiences. *"She was the worst boss."*
- Struggles to enjoy the good. "Summer is great, but it sucks that winter is coming."
- Lack of empathy. "Oh, you think you have it bad? What about . . ."
- Afraid of any risk. "I can't do that. Something bad always

happens when I try."

- Disinterested in solutions. "There's nothing that can be done."
- Rejects feedback or support. "I can't do that. It will never work."
- Lacks trust in others. "No one understands; therefore, I can never trust anyone."
- Cynical toward others' motives. "People are always out to get me."
- Narcissistic. "Pay attention to my problems. You should feel sorry for me."

If you can relate to any of this then please know you can alchemize a victim mentality into one of victor and survivor. Healing modalities such as **cultivating an abundance mindset, energy work, yoga, and being in nature** helped me to begin to fully integrate back into myself and therefore release a victim mentality. Other ways you can work to remove the mentality of victimization include the following twelve practices.

1. **Set powerful intentions.** These can be grounded in healing, reclaiming your power, and fully seeing yourself as both victim and survivor, for example.
2. **Utilize the power of the pause.** When you're asked to do something you don't have to do and are unsure if you want

to, you can use this to decide if you really want to do it. In the case of being triggered you can pause to reflect on what you're feeling and why, then process through the emotions so you can decide what's the best course of action before you respond.

3. **Reflect, reflect, reflect.** When triggered by others, honor your emotions fully, and ask yourself where this is coming from. What part of yourself is being called to heal in this moment of discomfort? What do you want to do to resolve this from an understanding that you, and you alone, are ultimately responsible for your emotions? And then engage when you're ready.

4. **Use affirmations to lean into new beliefs.** You can replace *"The world is against me,"* with *"The world is here to support me,"* for example.

5. **Set boundaries.** The dosage of our boundaries is the dosage of our love for self. Set boundaries so people know how to treat you. Don't make assumptions of what they should just know. Give them an opportunity to understand what they did and to fix it. Then enforce those boundaries when they're broken with tenacity. From there, you can decide how much grace is right-sized for the boundary that has been broken. I typically use the rule of three, but you can use whatever rule feels right for you.

6. **Accept what is.** Acceptance is one of the greatest gifts we

can give ourselves. As Maya Angelou said, "Believe people the first time." This allows you to be honest with yourself about what has happened and the fuel to decide from there what your best course of action is.

7. **Be kind to yourself.** Pay attention to the words you speak to yourself and out loud. Replace these with more loving words. Instead of, *"I'm unloveable,"* for example you can say, *"I'm loved."*

8. **Communicate what you need.** Don't expect people to know what you need. We help people discover how we want to be treated through what we express, and of course what we allow (see #5 again :)).

9. **Lean into self-compassion.** When you make a mistake, allow it to be just that–a mistake. Mistakes are part of the human condition. We are not our mistakes which means we need not be defined by them. We are accountable for them, yes, but not a slave to them. There is no need to judge the mistake. Instead, acknowledge what you've done and make a commitment to be better to yourself and others, and then keep it moving!

10. **Remember your power.** Although trauma can make you feel like you don't have any power, you are powerful beyond measure. Not only because you survived the loss but also simply because power is your birthright. By remembering you always have power, you are allowing

yourself to act from a place of empowerment.

11. **Be grateful.** There are endless things to be grateful for in your life. The more good you see, the more good you will have and the better you will feel. You can begin and end your day with gratitude and set an intention to be grateful throughout the day as well. Gratitude is one of the easiest ways to reconnect with your power.

12. **Be in service to others.** When we do good in the world, we not only feel better about ourselves, but we also feel like we're making a difference. And that's a pure power move!

As a licensed therapist and certified professional coach through the International Coaching Federation I would be remiss if I also didn't highlight the power of both healing modalities to overcome a victim mentality, as long as the practitioner is trauma and grief informed. A deep analysis of trauma and grief will help ensure that you are working with a professional who has the knowledge and skills to fully support you. You would assume that any therapist would be able to do this but the reality is our training doesn't include the depth it requires to be able to treat trauma and grief survivors in the most meaningful ways. This is why you should inquire about specialized training in the areas where you have experienced loss. The right professional can give you powerful insight into yourself, and help you curate a new vision for your life so loss doesn't serve as a barrier for you to design the life you want, the life you so deeply deserve.

Chapter 14
Real Liberation Comes From Forgiveness

Forgiveness is the fragrance that the violet sheds on the heel that has crushed it. -**Mark Twain**

The only sustainable, totally unhinged way to be free of trauma is to forgive the people who harmed us, along with ourselves if we have taken on the distorted burden of blame which is the case for so many survivors. In fact, it is more common than not for a trauma victim to blame themselves on some level for the abuse. Even in cases of divorce, which as we've explored is a trauma factor, research shows that one third of children blame themselves for up to six months after the divorce has occurred. In issues involving sexual assault that number is much higher and can last for the victim's lifetime.

"Internalized Blame of Self" is a natural coping defense that helps a child survive adverse circumstances in which she/he/they had no other resources to counter the abuse. What serves as a coping tool during trauma that occurs during adolescence becomes harmful during adulthood. As we become adults, these feelings of self-blame morph into self-sabotage which is one of the main drivers of depression, anxiety, and other mental health conditions. Of course we can be a victim of trauma during adulthood and experience feelings of self-blame as well. In other words, it's a natural part of the trauma process, and if we endure trauma as an adolescent, chances are the effects will be more pervasive.

There are many reasons why someone might be compelled to blame themselves for the trauma they endured. When the body is experiencing a traumatic event it will go into fight, flight, or freeze mode. More times than not, in issues of sexual assault, the body freezes which immobilizes the victim.

Dissociation is often coupled with the body's inability to move. A dissociative response in a person involves the brain numbing their five senses, allowing the body to experience a higher level of pain tolerance as a means to survive. Another way to think of this is the brain "checking out," which can look like one looking off into space, in the opposite direction of their attacker, in a numb state. When people are dissociative, reactions like shouting out for help or fighting back just aren't available to them. The two immobility responses (tonic or collapsed) involve the brain shutting down someone's ability to move or speak for the purpose of survival. During an assault, these immobility responses manifest as a person not fighting back because they literally can't physically move.

The night that I was gang raped at gun point, as I described earlier in the book, I completely dissociated. Although I tried to talk my way out of being raped, and I pondered jumping out the window when I was alone in the guest room, or running down the stairs from the bathroom and out the front door, fear crippled me. It was like I became a walking zombie. Right before the incident was about to happen the only thing I could do was cry. I had no words. And as I lay there and one by one they had their way with me, I refused to look at them but instead kept my head tilted in the opposite direction with my gaze focused on one spot on the wall. The only time my focus shifted was their thrusts or when I would periodically look at myself watching myself. My soul had left my body and was observing this horrific sight. She watched in sorrow and I watched her with stoicism. I was empty, hollow. This shifting focus from the ceiling and my soul who had escaped me, continued until the assault was complete. We then rejoined but now "we" were altogether different.

Due to this inability to move, the victim can sometimes blame themselves for not doing something, or doing something more to counter their attackers. Many questions may arise after the attack that are rooted in a sense of the victim somehow being responsible.

"Why did I go over to his house?"
"Why didn't I leave when I felt something was wrong?"
"Why didn't I scream?"
"Why didn't I tell someone?"
"Why didn't I go to the police?"
"Why did I let them get away with it?"

And the list goes on. This kind of thinking is completely unfair to the victim. Regardless of the answers to the questions, you didn't ask for the abuse nor was your brain, as I have illustrated, equipped to counter the abuse. Although we could argue there are lessons in everything, taking on any identity of responsibility for harm inflicted upon us by our attackers is ludicrous and does nothing to help us move forward.

Forgiveness says you are given another chance to make a new beginning. **-Desmond Tutu**

Self-forgiveness, like forgiving others, can help us to realize the full gift of healing. Even when we are responsible for harming others, or didn't make the "best" decisions, a practice of self-forgiveness can be deeply powerful. It's the balance between being accountable for your actions and not dwelling on those harmful actions. Nor becoming the judge that constantly makes you feel bad. It's an acknowledgement that part of the human experience is to make mistakes; so, when we do, we simply work to do better next time.

To forgive is to cease to feel resentment against someone who harmed us, including when that someone is us. The Therapeutic Stages of Forgiveness & Self Forgiveness developed by George Jacinto & Beverly Edwards provides a blueprint for how to move through the process of self-forgiveness.

Recognition: The first stage involves individuals realizing that self-forgiveness is an option that can liberate them from negative self-assessment. Recognition often occurs after a period of rumination, during which individuals experience emotions such as anger, guilt, blame, self-blame, depression, resentment, anxiety, regret, and grief resulting from unresolved issues.

Responsibility: In this stage, individuals accept responsibility for the incidents that require self-forgiveness. They gain insight and develop self-empathy by acknowledging their own imperfections.

Expression: The third stage involves expressing the feelings that have arisen due to self-blame during the rumination process. Individuals revisit these feelings with the intention of working through them and moving forward in life.

Re-Creating: The final stage centers on re-creating one's life. It requires individuals constructing a renewed self-image that integrates their past experiences coupled with the direction for the future. This stage empowers individuals to move forward with a sense of wholeness and purpose, incorporating their imperfections into their self-concept while striving to be the best versions of themselves.

Forgiving isn't something you do for someone else. It's something you do for yourself. It's saying, 'You're not important enough to have a stranglehold on me.' It's saying, 'You don't get to trap me in the past. I am worthy of a future.'-**Jodi Picoult**

In terms of our attackers, even when we get to the stage of acceptance in the grief process, we may still harbor negative feelings towards them which ultimately impedes our ability to fully move on. The only pathway to true liberation from trauma is to forgive.

There is a plethora of research on how forgiveness plays an essential role in trauma recovery, not to mention our overall health, including lowering the risk of heart attack, improving cholesterol levels and sleep, and reducing pain, blood pressure, anxiety, depression, and stress. Trauma survivors who participated in forgiveness-focused interventions showed reductions in shame and guilt. Further, forgiving others after trauma can facilitate meaning-making and contribute to post traumatic growth which is the positive development individuals can experience following a traumatic event. This results in a greater appreciation for life. On a final note, studies involving veterans have found that those most prone to forgive had lower depression and decreased symptoms of Post Traumatic Stress Disorder (PTSD), while harboring anger or desires for revenge is associated with higher levels of PTSD.

For me, forgiveness and compassion are always linked: how do we hold people accountable for wrongdoing and yet at the same time remain in touch with their humanity enough to believe in their capacity to be transformed? -**bell hooks**

In spite of all of the research that tells us forgiveness is good for us on a mind, body, spirit level, some trauma practitioners and survivors feel that it is something that lessens the magnitude of the trauma and its "right-sized" consequences. That's not what forgiveness is about at all. It's simply an acknowledgement of wanting to let go of the suffering caused by the burden of unforgiveness. Individuals who harm others still deserve their right-sized karma and everything that goes along with it. But we deserve to be free. We deserve to love again, trust again, dream again. We deserve joy, and peace, and an abundant life in its fullness, but we can't achieve that fully if we're harboring unforgiveness.

Further, as we practice forgiveness on a regular basis, studies have found individuals to be more satisfied with their lives and to have less depression, anxiety, stress, anger, and hostility. Whereas, people who hang on to grudges are more likely to experience severe depression and posttraumatic stress disorder, as well as other negative health conditions.

When a deep injury is done to us, we never recover until we forgive.
-Alan Paton

As cliche as it sounds, forgiveness is truly for us. Any negative emotions we harbor, especially for a long period of time, has major implications on our emotional, physical, and spiritual health. According to Karen Swartz, M.D., director of the Mood Disorders Adult Consultation Clinic at The Johns Hopkins Hospital, chronic anger puts you into a fight-or-flight mode, which results in numerous changes in heart rate, blood pressure, and immune response. "Those changes, then, increase the risk of depression, heart disease, and diabetes, among other conditions. Forgiveness, however, calms stress levels, leading to improved health." posits Swartz.

Forgiveness is not something that just happens. We set out to forgive because to choose anything other than that is to only harm ourselves. It is literally the equivalent of suffering on top of the suffering which is madness. We have already been harmed by the abuse and the lingering effects of it. Why not lessen the grip of unforgiveness by accepting what is, by seeing humanity even in the things that seem deeply inhumane on the surface? It's a conscious embodiment of the fact that we are all broken, and sometimes that brokenness nearly shatters us and the worlds of those around us.

To forgive is to set a prisoner free and discover that the prisoner was you. **-Lewis B. Smedes**

Freedom (forgiveness) is a choice just like being a prisoner (unforgiveness). The problem is many people don't know they're not free and because they don't know they're not free, they can't make the choice to be free. Acknowledging that any harboring of unforgiveness is the equivalent of being in bondage is the first step towards radical forgiveness. It is bondage because any form of negative emotions we hold onto actually harm us.

The Emotional Guidance Scale, developed by Abraham Hicks, measures twenty-two core emotions ranging from higher vibrational emotions, such as joy, appreciation, and love, and lower vibrational emotions, such as fear, despair, and powerlessness. The scale is as follows:

1. Joy/Appreciation/Empowerment/Freedom/Love
2. Passion
3. Enthusiasm/Eagerness/Happiness
4. Positive Expectation/Belief
5. Optimism
6. Hopefulness
7. Contentment
8. Boredom
9. Pessimism
10. Frustration/Irritation/Impatience
11. Overwhelment (feeling overwhelmed)
12. Disappointment
13. Doubt
14. Worry
15. Blame
16. Discouragement
17. Anger
18. Revenge
19. Hatred/Rage
20. Jealousy
21. Insecurity/Guilt/Unworthiness
22. Fear/Grief/Desperation/Despair/Powerlessness

Ultimately your attraction point is rooted in your emotional vibration. In other words, the more you can harness higher vibrational emotions, such as optimism and passion, versus lower-level emotions, such as revenge and jealousy, our lives will ultimately be better and we will feel better in the process.

The school of thought is that no matter what you've experienced in life, and no matter what is showing up in our worlds–both our inner world and our outer world–we understand the choice to choose how we are going to see things. We can either find the gifts, lessons, and beauty in the unfolding of life, or we can find despair, darkness, and chaos. Ultimately, the law of attraction teaches us that whatever we focus on is what expands. The more we can accept what is, from a neutral place, and find the plethora of things to be grateful for, based on the present state and what's to come, the more we will be in a state of joy and peace and the more we will attract our deepest desires with a level of ease. We'll explore how to utilize this tool and many other abundance mindset tips in the next chapter.

Forgiveness is an active process in which you make a conscious decision to let go of negative feelings whether the person deserves it or not. -**Karen Swartz, M.D.**

Forgiveness has to be desired by the person who was harmed by the trauma. If one chooses not to forgive, there is no judgment in that. My hope is however, we will get to a place of forgiveness because of what it does to set us free. Liberation is priceless. We don't have to wait for paradise during the crossover, if that's what we believe. We can choose paradise right now, and one of the ways we get there is by fully releasing those who have harmed us through the courageous act of forgiveness. Freedom is our birthright that we can reclaim through this deeply powerful act. Further research has found that forgiveness:

- Can be offered unconditionally regardless of the other person's remorse. As we've explored, since forgiveness is an act of you granting yourself your own freedom, regardless of the acknowledgment of the perpetrator, you can forgive them simply because you deserve to be free.
- Is not excusing, condoning, or ignoring harmful behavior. Forgiveness isn't about making the harm invoked upon you by someone else okay, but is about acknowledging that you deserve to be free. You can be in a space of justice to hold those who harmed you accountable for the damage they've done while also choosing to forgive for yourself, so you can move on fully with your life.
- Is different from reconciliation because it doesn't require that the forgiver renew their relationship with the wrongdoer.
- Doesn't require that the person who has caused the harm recognize their responsibility and work to change their behavior.

As I walked out the door toward the gate that would lead to my freedom, I knew if I didn't leave my bitterness and hatred behind, I'd still be in prison. -**Nelson Mandela**

Dr. Robert Enright, a pioneering researcher on forgiveness and the first to develop a comprehensive model of forgiveness, created a twenty step framework to help us understand the forgiveness process. The model condensed into four phases encompasses the following:

Uncovering Phase: This entails deep reflection on the way the trauma hurt you, not just at the time of the trauma but the aftermath. This is facing the trauma head on to unravel the depth of what the trauma took from you.

Decision Phase: There is recognition at this stage that the burden of carrying the load of unforgiveness is no longer serving you. Once you choose to forgive you can be open to the real possibility of forgiveness.

Working Phase: This is where the concerted work takes place to allow forgiveness to enter into our lives on a mind, body, and spirit level. From this place one works to understand their attacker as a driver of the trauma they caused. As empathy for the attacker ensues, an individual can soften enough to see the attacker as a victim, too–as more fully human. This is in no way about excusing the behavior, but simply understanding how the manifestation of trauma can cause someone to harm another. In this phase, one not only accepts the pain of what has happened, but begins to let go of resentment so as to offer their offender the gift of mercy, which eventually leads to the gift of freedom for oneself.

Outcome Phase: As the work of forgiveness continues, the hold of the pain associated with the trauma begins to dissipate, creating more room for joy, peace, and purpose to enter into our world. Meaning from the suffering can be derived during this phase as well. This doesn't mean that there isn't pain associated with the trauma anymore, in fact, there will probably always be residual suffering on some level. As we explored during the previous chapter, grief is a life-long process so there may be times across our life span where we experience moments of despair associated with the trauma. Because we've reached this phase though, we are able to move through those emotions rapidly so we can get back to feeling our best.

Though I was unaware of it at the time, that simple act of forgiveness was the beginning of an entirely new level of experiencing life for me.
-Wayne Dyer

Forgiveness is a practice we can utilize to let go of the small and big ways people harm us to experience more joy, peace, and ease, not to mention optimal health.

At its deepest level, forgiveness represents the belief that everything that happens to us, actually happens for us, in the sense that we can discover purpose in the harm. I also recognize that sometimes bad things simply just happen as described so powerfully in The Other Side of Yet, by Michelle D. Hord. In her book she also describes how you can find beauty after loss in spite of the depth of the loss. Forgiveness from this place is then seen as "radical" and part of the natural cycle of life.

Chapter 15

An Abundance Mindset Unlocks Evolutionary Liberation

When I think about creating abundance, it's not about creating a life of luxury for everybody on this planet; it's about creating a life of possibility. It is about taking that which was scarce and making it abundant.

-Peter Diamandis

The year that I started my consulting practice, long before I knew anything about abundance, some wild things happened that now I know for sure correlated to the energy I was putting into my desires. After five years, and reaching the glass ceiling at the not-for-profit housing organization where I worked, I took a job for a racial healing organization. I had followed the organization's work for several years, attending all sorts of training and events they hosted, and became well-acquainted with the director.

Months prior, I had been getting the feeling that something new was on the horizon, but I didn't know what. Then over the holiday break, the director called to schedule a lunch meeting to discuss a new position she thought might be a good fit for me. By the end of that lunch she offered me that position where I would mainly be responsible for facilitating several structural racism task forces. Although she couldn't pay me what I wanted initially, she said that after a few months of good work she would find the additional money. I had fallen in love with the organization and had a deep respect for their director, so it was a resounding yes from me.

Three months into my role, and being told consistently I was doing a stellar job by the director, based on my outputs and the buzz that had been building in the community about how much people enjoyed working with me, it was time for my quarterly review. Within minutes of the meeting, I felt as if I had been bamboozled. Not only did she rate me poorly across nearly every area in the review, she informed me she would be taking my structural racism task force work away and assigning me other projects. Additionally, the raise I had been expecting would not materialize. I asked questions to try and understand this astronomical shift, but it became clear quite quickly that no matter how hard I tried, there was nothing I could do to change her mind.

This woman whom I had admired for years, had morphed into someone I could no longer recognize. She was out to get me for a reason unbeknownst to me, and I was stuck to navigate through it until I could find something else. From then on, although I was cordial and professional, you could cut the tension in the office with a knife. On most days I would shut my door, cry silent tears, and then use the little energy I had left to lay the foundation for my consulting practice. I had launched my practice about a month before taking the position, and had been using my vacation time to work with the couple clients I had.

One of my new assignments was serving on the advisory

committee for the Battle Creek Children's Defense Fund (CDF) Freedom Schools program. Although this wasn't what I was looking for, I grew to love the program. I loved the intentionality, the culturally relevant approach, the books reflective of the lives of Black & Brown students, and the "call and response" - a practice derived from Africa. As part of that work, I was asked to create a social justice curriculum for middle schoolers who were in the program and deliver it over the summer. By the end of the summer I developed a tight bond with the instructor. I had no idea the program and instructor were about to drastically change my life.

During this time, I was also in my second class of graduate school, and had applied for a Thurgood Marshall Fellowship which I had been waitlisted for. This would cover the entire cost of my grad program, and then some. When I discussed being waitlisted with my graduate advisor and others, they urged me to forget about the fellowship considering the competitive nature of the program. They told me the chance of being moved from the waitlist would be slim to none. I listened to their concerns but I never lost hope in the possibilities.

Not long after, and for reasons I wasn't aware of, the director of the organization had a rapid departure. Thinking my experience and passion had prepared me for such a role, I applied, and was immediately told I wouldn't be considered. At that moment, something came over me, and I decided that it was time for me to sever ties with the organization, so I gave a nine-week notice. This would give them time to find a replacement and me time to better position myself to do consulting work full-time. Of course when I informed family and friends about the decision to leave to do consulting work full-time, they thought I was crazy. In spite of this, I knew it was the right decision, so I remained steadfast.

About a month later the middle school instructor called to see if I had an interest in co-founding a CDF Freedom Schools program in Kalamazoo. I said yes immediately. I saw first-hand how impactful the program had been and I couldn't wait for Black and Brown youth to experience it in my community. In a matter of about eight months, we secured a fiscal sponsor, a space, and applied for $90,000 in grant funding, but we wouldn't find out if we received the funding until a few days before my last day of being employed. A well-established organization, with ample resources, also expressed an interest in starting the program, but they said they didn't have time to successfully launch in the summer. We, on the other hand, never lost faith that we would have what we needed to launch on time, in spite of the fact we were just two young women on a mission.

Three days before my last day of employment, I received a phone call saying we obtained the funding we applied for–all $90,000 of it. The day before my last day I got a letter from Western Michigan University congratulating me on being awarded a Thurgood Marshall Fellowship. I had also secured a new client, and saved $9,000 from part-time consulting, so I was able to comfortably transition to consulting immediately after my departure.

That first year I made more money than my previous salary, year two my income doubled, and each year since I have experienced increased financial abundance as a result of my consulting work and passion projects, such as Be Well Beautiful Woman.

The key to abundance is meeting limited circumstances with unlimited thoughts. -**Marianne Williamson**

If we can adopt the idea that life is happening for us, even in the most dire situations, we can find the light. Being mistreated by my director quickly aligned me to the next chapter of my purpose. Having the courage to give that nine-week notice, in spite of not having anything concretely to transition into, was the best gift I gave myself. Choosing to not harbor resentment towards the director allowed me to keep my heart open. Fully embracing the new tasks I was given allowed me to see the beauty in the CDF Freedom Schools program. Choosing not to wallow in the way I was treated, the fact I wouldn't be making the money I had relied on, or that I was no longer doing the work I was initially hired for, allowed me to divert my energy to laying the foundation for Kalamazoo CDF Freedom Schools and building my consulting practice. Not allowing others' opinions to be my guide allowed me to stay in a constant state of peace. And having unwavering faith that all was going to work in my favor, kept me moving with gusto towards my goals.

But here is the thing, although that was a layered illustration of how Source/Universe/God/Creator can provide for us when we do the work and maintain a positive attitude in the process, good things had been coming my way for years.

Those early gifts looked much different, like being given the opportunity to be an assistant teacher at Kalamazoo Advantage Academy, a charter school that was located downtown. This was just a week after I spent the night in jail for falsifying information to a police officer, driving with no license, and driving under the influence. Before I was locked up I had been strongly contemplating turning my life around and had made some steps in the right direction. After that night though, I told myself I never wanted to go to jail again and things started shifting immediately. I was offered the job before my eighteenth birthday, which made me the youngest person on staff. And by the way, I wasn't even looking for such a role. My mother happened to be a recruiter and told the principal about me. We talked, and she offered me the job on the spot, in spite of divulging my recent run-in with the police. It was this experience that planted an early seed that eventually led me to a plethora of youth development and early childhood work.

Abundance is the process of letting go; that which is empty can receive. -**Bryant H. McGill**

When I first moved out on my own at the age of sixteen, I barely had enough money to pay my rent and owned very few belongings. For example, in the first apartment I had to furnish, I slept on a mattress with no headboard and frame, had one futon in the living room, and a pub style table with two chairs in the dining room. I didn't own a car until I was twenty-one, so at one point, I'd take the bus to my third shift job which wasn't on a bus line. I'd walk the roughly forty-five minutes to the mall to get on the bus and then go out to Kalamazoo Valley Community College to take classes. I'd take the bus home and get whatever rest I could before getting up to do it all over again. In fact, I was so broke, I obtained a mere $10 in food stamps which would at least provide one meal per month. I never borrowed a dime from anyone. Ever. I just made it work. And as a result, miraculously, my needs were always met, along with some wants, too.

In spite of the lack I had, I never focused on that. I just kept getting up and working towards change. I was grateful for the little that I had and, as a result, I increasingly had more to be grateful for. I worked extremely hard and remained positive. This is one of the principles of abundance, that no matter how little we have, no matter how much pain we've endured, finding the light in the midst of the darkness will help us see clearly enough to curate more light.

And although the pain of my childhood played out in the background in a myriad of ways, I wouldn't allow myself to get stuck in it. I still saw myself as the black sheep of my family but I didn't spend a lot of time and energy thinking about it. Nearly anytime I thought about being raped, it moved me to tears, I would cry and stay in forward motion. That experience, maybe more than any other, ripped me apart, but there wasn't anything I could do to erase what happened to me. So instead, I just kept putting one foot in front of the other.

I had lost things that I would never be able to name, and yet I had chosen to forgive it all. The burden of carrying the rape was enough. Holding on to any resentment towards my attackers only hurt me more. So about five years after the rape, I released them and anyone who caused me pain in connection with the rape: my therapist, the detectives, my mom, friends. I don't know how I knew it then, but I just knew that forgiving them was for myself. Although I didn't wish any of them harm, karma is going to do what karma does for all of us, so I could ultimately just let it be. It wasn't my battle to fight. From that place, my life gradually got better and better and better.

Why are you so enchanted by this world, when a mine of gold lies within you?-**Rumi**

The way we counter lack in any form, is to adopt an abundance mindset. According to Tony Robbins, an abundance mindset is the belief that there are enough resources in the world for everyone–and of being grateful for whatever the universe provides. It's often talked about in contrast with a scarcity mindset, or the belief that the world's resources are finite. An abundance mindset is rooted in optimism and possibilities coupled with labor, and the belief that we are worthy of receiving anything we desire. Abundance thinking is embedded in the unwavering belief that joy, peace, prosperity, and pleasure is your birthright. In other words, there is an inherent knowing that no lack exists, and because no lack exists, there is plenty for us all.

Remember, no more effort is required to aim high in life, to demand abundance and prosperity than is required to accept misery and poverty.
-Napoleon Hill

The psychology of scarcity on the other hand says that any time we focus on lack of any kind including money, time, relationships, and more, our mental bandwidth is adversely affected, according to Princeton University psychology and public affairs professor Eldar Shafir, PhD, who with Harvard University economist Sendhil Mullainathan, PhD, studies the topic of scarcity. Their research shows perceived scarcity can manifest in ongoing cognitive deficits and reinforced self-defeating actions.

Although poverty isn't a trauma factor, any form of lack, as described, creates scarcity which in the case of money, takes on the form of a poverty mindset. Alan Weiss, PhD, described poverty mindset as one that influences behaviors consistent with beliefs like, money shouldn't be spent, opportunities are limited, risk is dangerous, wealth isn't for you, and the list goes on. Fear of lack, that things never work out, and what you have can be taken away at any moment are also at the heart of scarcity. This may manifest itself in hoarding, being jealous of what other people have, not seeing your worth, being afraid to ask for more, and shaming others for believing they can have what they desire.

You are, at this moment, standing right in the middle of your own acres of diamonds.-**Earl Nightingale**

My first official encounter with abundance thinking came about through Pam Grout's E Squared more than seven years ago. I had to read the first chapter three times before I could move on because the thought of me being powerful in the way that Pam described was difficult to wrap my mind around. I had always believed that life was happening outside of myself and that it was simply my job to accept whatever life threw at me. Once I got through the first chapter I became open to the possibilities that I could use my mind to manifest things into my life. I proceeded with the experiments, and baby, let's just say my mind was blown.

When I did the first experiment, based on what Pam calls the Dude Abides Principle which explains that an invisible energy field of infinite possibilities is always available to us, I had to believe that I would manifest a gift within forty-eight hours. Within that period I got a speaking engagement for twice the fee they paid me the year before at the same conference. My next experiment was based on the Abracadabra Principle, which is connected to the universal law that everything you focus on expands. Once again, I'd have forty-eight hours to manifest something I specifically desired, but before I go into what happened, let me provide some context.

There was a potential client I had been vetting for months, and when I say months, I mean nine to be exact. In the consulting world this isn't necessarily unheard of, but typically from the time a consultation with a potential client takes place to the time they make a decision about working with you is more aligned with no more than ninety days. At the beginning of the year I decided I wanted to be debt free which required me to pay off the more than $60K in student loan debt I had racked up mainly during undergrad. I was making steady progress and as a result I was down to a $25,000 balance. Within hours of the forty-eight hour period ending, I received an email from the potential client saying they were ready to proceed with the engagement, and you know what their first payment was? Yep, $25,000.

I was so excited about the transformation I experienced after reading E Squared that I told everyone I knew about it. One of the earliest persons I recommended the book to manifested a judgeship and many other forms of abundance since that first contact with the book. Shortly after her appointment she wrote me this:

Hey Sis! Wanted to drop a note of appreciation and love. I was recently appointed to serve as a judge for the 8th District court. I start next month. As I began to reflect on this moment, I was reminded by spirit about the time we sat in your office and you told me about E2. That book truly changed my life and ushered me into a new spiritual path. It was that conversation that pushed me to leap beyond what I had been taught in my "churchy" upbringing and really tap into a new spiritual understanding and power that was within me. I drop this note to say thank you for letting spirit use you and for continuing to grow deeper into spiritual healing work. Know that even the small impressions you make ripple big. I don't think this moment would have come to me without the awakening of learning to truly manifest and to protect my energy. I would not have been open to other teachings and I certainly wouldn't have had the courage to leave the church to truly find God along this path. There are so many more experiences that happened since that meeting, but I want you to know how valuable and enlightening that moment was to me. You are an incredible force. Sending you a virtual hug! -**Honorable Alisa Parker Lagrone**

This is just one of the many people I know that have embraced their power to bring good into their lives by applying abundance principles. Many people go through life with no level of awareness of the power that Source/Universe/God/Creator has given them to bring in their deepest desires. Every thought we have either allows for things to come into our life that align with what we want, or brings things into our life that we don't want. As someone described to me recently, it's the difference between the flow of going downstream and the rough terrain of going upstream. In other words, the better we feel, the more life flows; the worse we feel the more life strains. This is why the most important thing we can do in life is to mind our thoughts. If we can interrupt negative thoughts before they begin to expand we can be in a fairly constant state of bliss and on the receiving end of many, many gifts that came to us with tremendous ease.

One thing I want to point out is Alisa's note about truly finding God. More often than not, we are brought up with a religious orientation that comes with being taught things that counter the idea we are powerful. So much so that we are always co-creating with Source/Universe/God/Creator. Everything in our world, from blessings to lessons, are there for us. But most people believe that life is happening to them rather than life is happening for them.

We have been told that God is ultimately powerful and we have to wait on God to get our needs and wants met. I'll never forget a friend of mine saying they had to wait on God to be healed. I pushed back and inquired why she thought she had to wait on God and she explained that God was the only one who can heal. I said quite the contrary, God has given us the power to heal ourselves and oftentimes while we're waiting on God, God is ultimately waiting on us. This is the epitome of free will. Although Source/Universe/God/Creator wants to give us all that our hearts truly desire, we have to make the decision to act in alignment towards what we say we want.

In The Abundance Book, John Randolph Price states, "The concept of all sufficiency was a building block of all philosophical and religious systems until the second century AD when the war against self-knowledge and self-reliance began." Randolph Price goes on to share that the Ancients taught us that to understand oneself was to understand God and through the process of stillness this truth would be revealed. He posits that through meditation, one could release the divine energy from within and transmute discord into harmony, ignorance to wisdom, fear into love, and lack into abundance. In other words, we are one with the Creator and when we get still enough we can tap into our Source-given power.

The Abundance Book describes how every religion across the globe that emphasized our oneness with God, the divinity of each individual, and the creative power of each soul to rise above limitation, were nearly erased from their teachings as a means to limit our perceived power. Yet certain passages regarding our birth-given power to generate prosperity in all forms still survived. In the New Testament for example, there are countless instances where we are told that not only are we powerful, but we also have free will. That means no matter how much we want something it will be impossible to get it without some work in that direction.

You the only person alive who holds the key to your healin'. So you take it and you run with it. And keep going even when your sun's hidden.
-Angel Haze

One of the challenges of having a spiritual leader, such as a priest or pastor, is that we will typically hold this person in such high regard that it diminishes the truth. The truth is we have a direct link to God, God is in us. We are God, we are truth, and we can seek truth–all within our own right. I recognize that church can be a source of strength for individuals, so my point isn't to take away from that. I'm only emphasizing that we have everything we need inside of ourselves to create a beautiful life. As Johann Wolfgang Von Goethe said, "As soon as you trust yourself, you will know how to live."

God isn't separate from us. Even when we are not operating from a place of love, openness, gratitude, or power, God is still with us. But the flow of energy that supports us in manifesting the life we want with ease isn't accessible. We attract things that cause us angst because of the angst we are feeling. Everything we transmit out, comes back. If we are operating in fear and other negative thoughts, and not from a place of abundance thinking, we will be unable to experience the fullness of life in the way we were intended to – rooted in love, peace, purpose, and pleasure. Another way to think about this is that when you are in your most optimal state you are most connected to Source/Universe/God/Creator. When you're most connected you feel your best, which makes it easier for you to manifest what you want.

You can become instantly successful with a simple thought, but long-lasting and pronounced success comes to those who renew their commitment to a mindset of abundance every minute of every hour of every day. -Bryant McGill

Let's take another look at the Emotional Guidance Scale created by Abraham Hicks to help you focus on how to manage your emotions. If your feelings are typically in the top five, your life is much easier and you are altogether more happy and grounded in peace. If, on the other hand, your emotions are typically in the bottom five, you probably feel pretty miserable much of the time, and the ability to manifest within those emotional states is nearly impossible. In other words, the better you feel, the more you receive, and with more ease.

1. Joy/Appreciation/ Empowerment/Freedom/Love
2. Passion
3. Enthusiasm/Eager/Happiness
4. Positive Expectation/Belief
5. Optimism
6. Hopefulness
7. Contentment
8. Boredom
9. Pessimism
10. Frustration/Irritation/ Impatience

11. Overwhelmed

12. Disappointment

13. Doubt

14. Worry

15. Blame

16. Discouragement

17. Anger

18. Revenge

19. Hatred/Rage/Jealousy

20. Insecurity/Guilt/Unworthiness

21. Fear/Grief/Desperation/Despair/Powerlessnes

You never change things by fighting against the existing reality. To change something, build a new model that makes the old model obsolete.
-Buckminster Fuller

So the key is to pay attention to your thoughts all the time. As Joyce Meyer said, "to think about what you're thinking about." Then reframe those negative thoughts into positive thoughts that are going to make you feel better, over and over and over again. Take for example, you get stuck in traffic. Instead of being angry about it, go into full acceptance mode and say something to yourself like, "Thank you—I have no idea why I'm stuck in traffic, but thank you. I'm trusting how my life is unfolding."

Getting into a place of acceptance allows you to instantly be in a state of peace. The Buddha said that suffering is rooted in our inability to accept what is, so the sooner we can accept, whether we agree with it or not, the sooner we can get back to feeling better, and the sooner we can get reconnected to abundant flow.

Research supports that we have on average 60,000 thoughts a day, and that 90% of these thoughts are on autopilot. This gives us countless opportunities to be mindful about our thoughts because our thoughts become our emotions, and our emotions become actions. What we say and think about ourselves and other people ultimately matter. The more loving our thoughts can be towards ourselves and others, the better we feel, and the more the gifts of life appear in ways we desire and oftentimes are even better.

Acknowledging the good that you already have in your life is the foundation for all abundance. -**Eckhart Tolle**

Having an abundance mindset creates flow in your life, causing you to not have to work as hard. When I first started my business I was doing the most, like co-founding Kalamazoo CDF Freedom Schools, grad school, operating my business, being a mom, and so much more. I was working so hard there were times when I would just break down and cry because I was so exhausted. Not to mention I was obesely overweight, barely slept, and my hair had started thinning.

One day my mother asked me what I was running towards. At the time the question seemed odd, but now I get what she meant. Her query was really about what I was trying to prove. For years people said I wouldn't amount to anything. As a young teen, my mother would get angry at me and say that I was just like my father. I wasn't clear about what she meant, but I knew the context wasn't good. By the time I was seventeen, so many people had written me off–teachers, my therapist, family, friends–that part of my intense labor was about proving to them, on a subconscious level, that they were wrong.

This takes me to my next point. Take inventory of what is driving you to do what you're doing. Real worth comes from the inside out which means no amount of labor or accomplishments will ever fill the void of feeling unworthy. The only thing that can make you feel worthy is yourself. External affirmation feels good, but it's not sustainable. Not to mention, we should become so clear about who we are that whether we get outside affirmation or not, it will have no bearing on how we see ourselves. We all are worthy just because we are here. We don't have to do anything to prove our worthiness. Thanks to The Four *Agreements* by Don Miguel Ruiz, one of the most valuable lessons I have learned is not to take anything personal, even when people have intentions to harm me. If I know the truth of who I am, whether people love me or hate me shouldn't matter. The only thing that ultimately matters is how I see myself.

This is why cultivating an abundance mindset is so important to our well-being. Not only should you have loving thoughts/words about yourself, you should also be mindful of the words of others that you accept as truth—because both will shape your life.

People with a scarcity mentality tend to see everything in terms of win-lose. There is only so much; and if someone else has it, that means there will be less for me. The more principle-centered we become, the more we develop an abundance mentality, the more we are genuinely happy for the successes, well-being, achievements, recognition, and good fortune of other people. We believe their success adds to. . . rather than detracts from . . . our lives. **-Stephen Covey**

Tenaciously being mindful about who we allow to take up stock in our lives is an important practice. As a pastor once said, whoever has your ear is who has your heart. And even when those in your circles project their stuff onto you, through the cultivation of an abundance mindset you can counter their words through the steadfast truth you have about yourself.

If we want to live well, if we want to live abundantly in every way, then we have to be willing to alchemize our trauma into abundance. By honoring the cycle of grief, forgiveness, and continuously working towards abundance thinking, you give yourself the gift of having bountiful joy, peace, purpose, and pleasure every single day, not to mention financial prosperity.

An abundance mindset allows you to say yes to yourself, fully honoring every aspect of who you are, what ignites you, and what you've been through. It's these practices, kept at the forefront of your life, that allow you to work in a flow state–which allows things to simply come to you. From this place you don't have to work as hard because one of the universal laws is that what you are seeking is seeking you. Yes, we put in the work towards what it is that we want, but as we trust Source/Universe/God/Creator, and believe that we are worthy, we will more easily, and rapidly, be able to bring the things we want into our lives. Here is a formula that I created shortly after I started my abundance mindset journey that keeps abundance at the forefront of my life.

BELIEVE+ASK+TRUST+WORK+GRATITUDE+WAIT = ABUNDANCE FLOW

Believe is about knowing the truth of who you are and that simply because of your birth, you are an heir to all the Source/Universe/God/Creator has to offer, which has no bound. You don't have to do anything to earn your worthiness, you are simply worthy because you're here.

Ask is about going after anything you want in this lifetime, whether it be money, or nice cars, luxurious experiences, aligned relationships, good health, absolutely anything–both the big and the small. We are always asking for things, whether we are conscious of this or not. Each thought is a form of asking which is why we have to ensure that our thoughts are loving towards ourselves and others.

The more we can do this, the more we can keep our channels clear for receiving what we desire. So go ahead and ask for all you want through prayer, journaling, affirmations, conversations, visioning, and more, and know that in time you will receive it.

Trust encompasses your belief that you will receive what you desire regardless of how removed from it you are right now, or how bleak your circumstances might seem. When we have faith, we are unshakable in our belief that the things we want will come to fruition.

Work entails the things we do to align with exactly what we want. We can say that we want something countless times but if we are not taking action that supports what we want then we will be hard pressed to receive it. The process of co-creation requires us to work in the co-curating process with Source/Universe/God/Creator. If all you're doing is "wishing up" what you want and not working towards it then you are literally sending a message that you aren't really ready to receive what you want. The energy that you put into something gets matched with life force energy towards your desires. If there is no action, there is little support because of the law of labor which says when you work there is eventually a pay off. As Ask & It Is Given authors Esther & Jerry Hicks say, "The Universe won't send us what we want until we are fully ready to receive it."

Gratitude is the process of being thankful for the bountiful life we already have, and the additional bounty that is coming. It is about giving thanks in all things, and seeing the gifts in even the darkest moments. It is our ability to look around at our lives and see endless things to be thankful for from the breeze coming in through a window, to the smell of a candle, to the colors in nature. It is about being thankful about the small things and the big things. But it is also about being grateful for what's to come, as if it is already here. Additionally acknowledging the gifts and support you receive from people by virtue of the Source/Universe/God/Creator. Because what we focus on expands, the more we lean into gratitude, the more things will come into our lives that we have to be thankful for. Gratitude in itself creates a flow state.

Wait is the belief in the divine timing of things. It is the inherent belief that all things will manifest in perfect timing. Knowing that when a door closes, another more optimal door is on the horizon. Understanding that the things you desire will come to you when your heart, mind, and soul are ready. When you're in a state of consciousness through the cultivation of your inner well-being, that allows you to see and hear the way Source/Universe/God/Creator is guiding you towards what you want–along with enough courage to say yes when aligned opportunities are presented to us.

It's also important to understand that people are the main way that Source/Universe/God/Creator brings us abundance which is why it's critically important to ask for help and be ready to receive it. And of course be grateful for it when it comes your way.

I'm excited to know about all the ways your life will change as a result of you applying the practices I've outlined in this chapter. No matter where you are in your journey, no matter how little you have in the material world, or how much trauma you've endured, applying these principles consistently will drastically change your life. In Pam's follow up book to E Squared, E Cubed, she highlights countless stories of people's manifestation power. And I imagine if you searched for abundance on the internet you would find ample evidence of what I've outlined. Let's get this abundance! We oh, so, deserve it.

DEMARRA WEST

Demarra West, author of Me Too: A Therapist's Journey to Heal, Find Liberation, & Joy became a therapist more than a decade ago. Although she knew that her attraction to therapy was rooted in the tumultuous childhood she had, she was convinced that was in the past, and never really saw that she too, had immense healing to do

That came to fruition a few years ago when she turned to holistic healing practices to support her work with Be Well Beautiful Woman, a global wellness company dedicated to helping all women heal and liberate, especially those most in need,

It was those same practices that helped her face the dark parts of herself that trauma had created and alchemize those parts into becoming more of what she was always created to be.

Now she lives a full vibrant life on a mind, body, spirit level, and is tapping into the birth given joy, peace, and prosperity we were all meant to experience.

In addition to being a therapist, Demarra is certified in trauma sensitive yoga, a Reiki master, a professional certified coach, and trained in a myriad of healing modalities that she uses to support her healing first, and then those she is privileged to serve.

www.demarrawest.com
info@demarrawest.com

www.ingramcontent.com/pod-product-compliance
Lightning Source LLC
Chambersburg PA
CBHW020435130626
46549CB00001B/154